FREE PRESS
BUSINESS

DATE DUE

APR 07 2010

NOR
FLOF
26
WES
D1262138

ALSO BY SETH GODIN

Survival is Not Enough

The Big Red Fez

Unleashing the Ideavirus

Permission

Marketing™

Turning Strangers into

Friends, and Friends into

Customers

SETH GODIN

FREE PRESS
BUSINESS

This edition first published in Great Britain
by Simon & Schuster UK Ltd, 2002
A Viacom Company

1 3 5 7 9 10 8 6 4 2

Simon & Schuster UK Ltd
Africa House
64–78 Kingsway
London WC2B 6AH

www.simonsays.co.uk

Simon & Schuster Australia
Sydney

A CIP catalogue record for this book
is available from the British Library

ISBN 0–7432–2142–7

Printed and bound in Great Britain by
The Bath Press, Bath

This book is dedicated to Jerry Shereshewsky, visionary, apostle to the uninformed, brave marketer. Yoyodyne wouldn't have developed without him, and this book wouldn't have been written without his insights and agita.

CONTENTS

Foreword

by Don Peppers
coauthor, *The One to One Future*
founder, marketing 1:1, inc.

I predict that businesses all over the world will soon be familiar with most of the concepts outlined in this book. Sales and marketing people everywhere will soon be talking about the very commonsense principles of "Permission Marketing" and how best to put these principles to work for their own businesses.

To prove the accuracy of my prediction, I'll ask you to consider your own hectic life. The truth is, your whole problem comes down to a question of time and energy, doesn't it? Technically, life is easier for you than it was for your parents, because so much of the drudge work is now done by machines. But for some reason you're busier than ever, isn't that right? And doesn't it seem as though every day you get still busier?

How can this be? Simple. Because there are so many more claims on your attention, that's why. You're already overloaded with an embarrassment of opportunities to absorb your time and expend your funds doing things, watching things, using things. But every day even more opportunities are presented to you. So now when you decide to spend an hour surfing the Web, the first thing researchers want to know is: Hey, where did that extra *hour* come from, anyway?

It came out of your life, that's where. You made a tough choice. Decided to use an irreplaceable hour of your life cruising the Net rather than watching one of the 115 channels on the tube, or answering one of the 25 e-mail messages stacked in your queue, or driving out for a snack at one of the 30 fast-food restaurants located within a few miles of your home, or sunning at the pool, or playing Scrabble with your teenage daughter.

Face it: Your attention—the time you have available to "pay attention"—is an increasingly scarce resource. And, in any free economy, when resources become scarcer they command higher prices.

Now, to some of us this might appear to be a simple statement of economic principle. To Seth Godin, it's also a business opportunity.

The basic idea of "Permission Marketing" is very simple: Each of us is born with only a certain amount of time on this earth, and figuring out how to use it wisely is one of life's primary activities. "Paying attention" to something—anything—is, in fact, a conscious act, requiring conscious effort. So one way to sell a consumer something in the future is simply to get his or her permission in advance. You'll do this by engaging the consumer in a dialogue—an interactive relationship, with both you and the customer participating. Rather than simply *interrupting* a television show with a commercial or barging into the consumer's life with an unannounced phone call or letter, tomorrow's marketer will first try to gain the consumer's consent to participate in the selling process.

Perhaps the consumer will give his permission because he is volunteering to learn more about a particular product or class of products. Or perhaps you'll actually offer some type of payment or benefit in return for the consumer's permission.

In a noninteractive world this would be the kind of crazy, totally impractical idea that you might be tempted to chalk up to the idle musings of an overimaginative marketing geek. But the age of interactivity has actually arrived. It came suddenly, while no one was looking, and interactivity changed the rules.

The technology of interactivity has two quite different implications for businesses. On the one hand, because consumers can gain access to information faster and more simply than ever before, many marketers are finding their products "commoditized" and their margins squeezed. You can use the Web to buy a new General Motors car for as little as $50 over dealer invoice. Or you can buy a thousand shares of General Motors stock for a total commission of as little as $7.95. While this sounds like great news for consumers, clearly one of interactivity's immediate implications for business is that margins are going to get hammered and customer loyalty will be harder to come by.

But interactivity can also empower a business to engage its consumer customers in individual dialogues, developing relationships with each of them that grow stronger with time. Not only can this strategy shield a business from being commoditized, it can also provide a valuable service to consumers—a service, moreover, that might easily be worth more than access to the latest, most accurate price comparisons on a commodity product.

Engaging a consumer in a dialogue is something that

business owners used to do in the old days—before assembly-line production, mass distribution, and mass media advertising. In the old days selling was a kinder, gentler process, and it was based on the willing participation of the consumer. It was only the arrival of the mass production economy that changed all this. The modern economy was defined in terms of assembly-line production of standardized products, mass distribution of these products to consumers in a wide geographic area, and mass media vehicles to carry standardized advertising messages. Under these conditions it became irresistibly cost-efficient to broadcast the same message to every consumer, rather than bearing the cost of engaging any single consumer in a separate, individual dialogue.

Today, however, because of interactive technology, it has become cost-efficient once again to conduct individual dialogues, even with millions of consumers—one customer at a time.

Interactive technology means that marketers can inexpensively engage consumers in one-to-one relationships fueled by two-way "conversations"—conversations played out with mouse clicks on a computer, or touch-tone buttons pushed to signal an interactive voice response unit, or surveys completed at a kiosk. The point is that consumers can, once again, be *involved* in the marketing process. Marketing in an interactive world is a collaborative activity—with the marketer helping the consumer to buy and the consumer helping the marketer to sell.

As a business, if you do it right, the dialogue and involvement of a customer will lead to customer loyalty, for *that* customer. The more the customer is engaged—the more he or she has collaborated with you to fashion the service you are rendering or the product you are selling—the more likely the customer will be to remain loyal to you, rather than going to the trouble of switching this collaborative activity to one of your competitors.

For the business, this might seem like a lot of effort just to sell another quarter's worth of goods. It is. But there is no viable alternative, because the mass production economy has basically been tapped out. You already know this, if you just think about what your own life is like as a consumer within that economy.

As a consumer, you now inhabit an endlessly expanding universe of new offers, urgent solicitations, price-off promotions, and money-back guarantees. This is the mass production economic system carried to its logical extreme—businesses all trying to find more customers for an ever-widening array of more specialized and innovative products and services. In order to sell this vast arsenal of products, marketers all over the world soak up every square inch of space, every extra second of time, and they paste their sales messages into those nooks and crannies, hoping you'll encounter them. So, as a consumer your life is now filled to overflowing with this previously unimaginable variety of opportunities, choices, and assorted messages—all calling for decisions on your part, even if the only "action" you take is to pay attention for an instant. And make no mistake about it, your constant attention is demanded. Every idle moment you possess is seen by some business somewhere as an opportunity to interrupt you and demand more of your attention.

Marketers want to get their messages in front of you. They *must* get their messages in front of you, just to survive. The only problem is—do you really *want* more marketing messages?

Interactivity allows a business to break this vicious cycle. With cost-efficient interactive technologies now available, businesses can actually take a step back and secure their customers' permission to sell them things—to get them to pay attention to their selling messages. A business can now *ask* a consumer directly if he'd like more information and then deliver it. A business can now *reward* a consumer for receiving and acknowledging its message, ensuring that the consumer's own interest is served by learning about a new product or service.

There are lots and lots of ways to do this. Offer a coupon or a cash incentive. Play a game. Accumulate points. Sponsor a contest or a drawing. But whatever you do, however you do it, if you get your prospect's permission to sell to him, you have won a valuable asset, an asset no competitor can take from you. You have won the prospect's cooperation and participation. He and you are now collaborating.

So yes, my prediction is that companies all over the globe will be embracing Permission Marketing. They will embrace it both as an offensive marketing weapon, to steal customers from their competitors, and as a defensive measure, to avoid the kind of commoditization represented by e-commerce.

For any reader who wants to know how to compete in an interactive universe of World Wide Web sites, call centers, and sales force automation tools, stay tuned. If you want to avoid the e-commerce trap of commoditization and margin pressure, then this book's for you. If you want just to understand better the kinds of marketing relationships that are most likely to develop in the age of interactivity, then read on.

Anyone else, read a different book. You've got lots of other things you need to do anyway, right?

Introduction

I wasted a lot of Harvard University's endowment. More than $6 million, to be specific. And everyone around me applauded.

In 1983 Spinnaker Software emerged as the best-funded software start-up in history. With more than $17 million in venture money (including about $6 million from the sages at Harvard), Spinnaker set out to invent an entire genre—educational computer games for kids.

As one of a handful of brand managers at Spinnaker, my job (at the tender age of twenty-three) was to spend millions of dollars advertising our new products. Amazingly enough, this little start-up ranked among the two hundred largest advertisers in the country in 1984.

Armed with millions of dollars of ad money, I ran ads in *People* and dozens of other magazines. We had constant discussions about how to make the move to television and, of course, found ourselves invited to attend the U.S. Open and other great advertising shmoozefests.

The good news was that the advertising bought us distribution. We were picked up by Radio Shack, Lechmere, Target,

17

and Kmart. Within a year we were the leader in a zero-billion-dollar market.

The bad news was that we had no evidence at all that our advertising was actually working. No proof that the millions of dollars we were spending were doing anything more than buying fancy cars for the commissioned salespeople and generating fear among our competitors.

It was a great gig, but after sixty products and some great experiences, I decided to go into the book business. There, once again, I got a firsthand ringside seat at a waste jamboree, a huge bonfire of money spent with no return on traditional advertising.

Giant companies were spending millions of dollars to advertise a product on the network television coverage of the Olympics. Publishers with established brand-name authors had no idea which individuals were buying their books and had to start their marketing and promotions from scratch every time a new book was launched. Huge conglomerates were publishing hundreds of books a year but weren't cultivating a loyal audience, a brand name, or a scalable way of introducing new products.

What I had suspected at Spinnaker was proven true. Advertising wasn't working very well. It wasn't easily measured or tested. It wasn't predictable. And it was expensive.

For the last six years I've been a student of how companies deal with advertising and a practitioner of how they might do it with more success. I've watched with amusement as Excite ran million-dollar campaigns on *Seinfeld*—overpromoting a product before its time—and I've watched with despair as truly great products have disappeared because of a complete lack of promotion.

In 1990 the folks at Prodigy (a company that will be remembered as being years ahead of its time) hired my colleagues and me to build a promotion for their fledgling online service. Prodigy had two significant problems. The first was that it cost them hundreds of dollars to get a new member, yet the average member was staying only a few months before quitting the service. The second was that they were charging a flat fee, but many customers were using the service so much that Prodigy was actually losing money on their very best users.

Into this maelstrom we threw Guts®. Guts was one of the very first online promotions (it predated the World Wide Web by more than four years), and today, nearly a decade later, it's still one of the largest online promotions ever run. (And it continues to run online.)

More than 3 million people ended up participating in this promotion. If you entered it, you were *half* as likely to quit Prodigy as other members who didn't. Amazingly enough, you could tell when the new weekly version of the promotion was launched on Wednesdays, because usage of the entire Prodigy network would increase measurably.

Like a blind squirrel stumbling onto an acorn, we had accidentally discovered some really big insights. These successes led to promotions for AOL, Delphi, eWorld (Apple), Microsoft, and CompuServe. Along the way, I was lucky enough to be in a fast-moving advertising test laboratory.

The promotions we built for each online service did exactly what they were supposed to do. They increased usage, and they cut churn.

A couple of years ago, after forming a company to build the technology and, more important, the techniques necessary to do these extraordinarily successful promotions, I realized that my journey was a metaphor for what millions of marketers at millions of companies were doing, or were about to do. I'd gone from spending oodles of money in traditional advertising to building something completely different, vastly more efficient, and measurably more effective. We'd honed the idea of Permission Marketing.

In this book I'd like to challenge your preconceived notions about what marketing and advertising is and should be and put it back together in a way that works in our new networked world. The concepts are pretty simple, but they are by no means obvious.

My colleagues at Yoyodyne (the leading direct marketing company on the Internet) have been unrelenting in their mission to bring this message to major brands around the country. We've spoken at hundreds of conferences and gone on thousands of sales calls. We've been insulted by placeholder marketers who had salaries greater than their budgets and who enjoyed pulling the wings off flies like us. We've survived Java and Shockwave and MSN and multibillion-dollar investments designed to turn the Web into TV.

Technology is changing the world's approach to advertising. The Direct Marketing Association no longer ignores the Web—in fact, they devote whole conferences to it. E-mail has become a way of life, too. According to the American Management Association, more than half of all business executives rely on e-mail. A Catholic bishop based in New York was even quoted as saying, "If Jesus were walking the earth today, I'm convinced He would have an e-mail address."

If you believe that the Internet changes everything, you will readily appreciate this book. The feudal lords who counted on conquest of the New World five hundred years ago were blown away when they discovered that the old rules didn't work anymore—the product of their heavily financed expeditions turned out to be their own destruction. The New World eclipsed the Old World. Like a huge echo in a canyon, the sound waves the Old World sent out returned to eliminate their role in the world. Without the money the royalty of Europe spent to develop the United States, our country would never have developed into the world power that now eclipses them.

The Internet is going to change marketing before it changes almost anything else, and old marketing will die in its path. The marketers who funded the explosive growth of the Internet are going to be the first to be destroyed. Their experiments and hype and sizzle will open the eyes of consumers, but then these same consumers will realize that they don't need the old rules anymore.

If you don't believe that the Internet will change everything, you still need this book. You might be right, after all, but that won't change the fact that the overwhelming clutter in the marketplace has made traditional advertising almost worthless for most marketers. You need something that works, and as the examples in this book will demonstrate,

Permission Marketing works for companies big and small. It works online and offline, for consumers and for the business-to-business market.

Increasingly, there are only two kinds of companies: brave and dead. I hope that this book finds you in the first category. Let me know what you think!

SETH GODIN
Santa Clara, California

POSTSCRIPT

As this book goes to press, Yoyodyne has accepted an offer to be acquired by Yahoo!, the largest independent site on the Internet. After spending years developing and implementing many of the techniques described in this book, my colleagues and I now have the opportunity to apply our learning on a much larger scale. You can contact me at Seth@permission.com for an update on what the future holds for permission marketing online.

ONE

The Marketing Crisis That Money Won't Solve

You're not paying attention. Nobody is.

IT'S NOT YOUR FAULT. It's just physically impossible for you to pay attention to everything that marketers expect you to—like the 17,000 new grocery store products that were introduced last year or the $1,000 worth of advertising that was directed exclusively at *you* last year.

Is it any wonder that consumers feel as if the fast-moving world around them is getting blurry? There's TV at the airport, advertisements in urinals, newsletters on virtually every topic, and a cellular phone wherever you go.

This is a book about the attention crisis in America and how marketers can survive and thrive in this harsh new environment. Smart marketers have discovered that the old way of advertising and selling products isn't working as well as it used to, and they're searching aggressively for a new, enterprising way to increase market share and profits. Permission Marketing is a fundamentally different way of thinking about advertising and customers.

THERE'S NO MORE ROOM FOR ALL THESE ADVERTISEMENTS!

I remember when I was about five years old and started watching television seriously. There were only three main channels—2, 4, and 7, plus a public channel and UHF channel for when you were feeling adventuresome. I used to watch *Ultraman* every day after school on channel 29.

With just five channels to choose from, I quickly memorized the TV schedule. I loved shows like *The Munsters,* and I also had a great time with the TV commercials. Charlie the Tuna, Tony the Tiger, and those great board games that seemed magically to come alive all vied for my attention. And they got it.

As I grew up, it seemed as though everyone I met was part of the same community. We saw the same commercials, bought the same stuff, discussed the same TV shows. Marketing was in a groove—if you invented a decent product and put enough money into TV advertising, you could be pretty sure you'd get shelf space in stores. And if the ads were any good at all, people bought the products.

About ten years ago I realized that a sea change was taking place. I had long ago ceased to memorize the TV schedules, I was unable to keep up with all the magazines I felt I should be reading, and with new alternatives like Prodigy and a book superstore, I fell hopelessly behind in my absorption of media.

I found myself throwing away magazines unopened. I was no longer interested enough in what a telemarketer might say to hesitate before hanging up. I discovered that I could live without hearing every new Bob Dylan album and that while there were plenty of great restaurants in New York City, the ones near my house in the suburbs were just fine.

The clutter, as you know, has only gotten worse. Try counting how many marketing messages you encounter today. Don't forget to include giant brand names on T-shirts, the logos on your computer, the Microsoft start-up banner on your monitor, radio ads, TV ads, airport ads, billboards, bumper stickers, and even the ads in your local paper.

For ninety years marketers have relied on one form of advertising almost exclusively. I call it Interruption Marketing. Interruption, because the key to each and every ad is to interrupt what the viewers are doing in order to get them to think about something else.

INTERRUPTION MARKETING—THE TRADITIONAL APPROACH TO GETTING CONSUMER ATTENTION

Almost no one goes home eagerly anticipating junk mail in their mailbox. Almost no one reads *People* magazine for the ads. Almost no one looks forward to a three-minute commercial interruption on must see TV.

Advertising is not why we pay attention. Yet marketers must make us pay attention for the ads to work. If they don't interrupt our train of thought by planting some sort of seed in our conscious or subconscious, the ads fail. Wasted money. If an ad falls in the forest and no one notices, there is no ad.

You can define advertising as the science of creating and placing media that interrupts the consumer and then gets him or her to take some action. That's quite a lot to ask of thirty seconds of TV time or twenty-five square inches of the newspaper, but without interruption there's no chance for action, and without action advertising flops.

As the marketplace for advertising gets more and more cluttered, it becomes increasingly difficult to interrupt the consumer. Imagine you're in an empty airport, early in the morning. There's hardly anyone there as you stroll leisurely toward your plane.

Suddenly someone walks up to you and says, "Excuse me, can you tell me how to get to gate seven?" Obviously you weren't hoping for, or expecting, someone to come up and ask this question, but since he looks nice enough and you've got a spare second, you interrupt your train of thought and point him on his way.

Now imagine the same airport, but it's three in the afternoon and you're late for your flight. The terminal is crowded with people, all jostling for position. You've been approached five times by various faux charities on your way to the gate, and to top it all off you've got a headache.

Same guy comes up to you and asks the same question. Odds are, your response will be a little different. If you're a New Yorker, you might ignore him altogether. Or you may stop what you were doing, say "Sorry," and then move on.

A third scenario is even worse. What if he's the fourth, or the tenth, or the one hundredth person who's asked you the same question? Sooner or later you're going to tune out the interruptions. Sooner or later it all becomes background noise.

Well, your life is a lot like that airport scene. You've got too much to do and not enough time to get it done. You're being accosted by strangers constantly. Every day you're exposed to more than four hours of media. Most of it is optimized to interrupt what you're doing. And it's getting increasingly harder and harder to find a little peace and quiet.

The ironic thing is that marketers have responded to this problem with the single worst cure possible. To deal with the clutter and the diminished effectiveness of Interruption Marketing, *they're interrupting us even more!*

That's right. Over the last thirty years advertisers have dramatically increased their ad spending. They've also increased the noise level of their ads—more jump cuts, more in-your-face techniques—and searched everywhere for new ways to interrupt your day.

Thirty years ago clothing did not carry huge logos. Commercial breaks on television were short. Magazines rarely had three hundred pages of ads (as many computer magazines do today). You could even watch PBS without seeing several references to the "underwriter."

As clutter has increased, advertisers have responded by increasing clutter. And as with pollution, because no one owns the problem, no one is working very hard to solve it.

Consumers Are Spending Less Time Seeking Alternative Solutions

In addition to clutter, there's another problem facing marketers. Consumers don't need to care as much as they used to. The quality of products has increased dramatically. It's increased so much, in fact, that it doesn't really matter which car you buy, which coffee maker you buy, or which shirt you buy. They're all a great value, and they're all going to last a good long while.

We've also come a long way as consumers. Ninety years ago it was unusual to find a lot of brand-name products in a consumer's house. Ninety years ago we made stuff, we didn't buy it. Today, however, we buy almost everything. Canned goods. Bread. Perked coffee. Even water. As a result, we already have a favorite brand of almost everything. If you like your favorite brand, why invest time in trying to figure out how to switch?

We're not totally locked in, of course. It wasn't too long ago that cake mix was a major innovation. Just a few years ago we needed to make major decisions about which airline was going to be our supplier of frequent flier miles. And today, if you're going to get health care, you've got to make a serious choice. But more often than not, you've already made your decisions and you're quite happy with them.

When was the last time someone launched a major new manufacturer of men's suits? Or a large nationwide chain of department stores? Or a successful new nationwide airline? Or a fast-food franchise? It can be done, certainly, but it doesn't happen very often. One of the reasons it's such a difficult task is that we're pretty satisfied as consumers.

If the deluge of new products ceased tomorrow, almost no one would mind. How much more functional can a T-shirt get? Except for fast-moving industries like computers, the brands we have today are good enough to last us for years and years. Because our needs as consumers are satisfied, we've stopped looking really hard for new solutions.

Yet because of the huge profits that accrue to marketers who *do* invent a successful new brand, a new killer product, a new category, the consumer is deluged with messages. Because it's not impossible to get you to switch from MCI to Sprint, or from United Airlines to American Airlines, or from Reebok to Nike, marketers keep trying. It's estimated that the average consumer sees about one million marketing messages a year—about 3,000 a day.

That may seem like a lot, but one trip to the supermarket alone can expose you to more than 10,000 marketing messages! An hour of television might deliver forty or more, while an issue of the newspaper might have as many as one hundred. Add to that all the logos, wallboards, junk mail, catalogs, and unsolicited phone calls you have to process every day, and it's pretty easy to hit that number. A hundred years ago there wasn't even a supermarket, there wasn't a TV show, and there weren't radio stations.

Mass Media Is Dead. Long Live Niche Media!

Technology and the marketplace have also brought the consumer a glut of ways to be exposed to advertising. When the FCC ruled the world of television, there were only three networks and a handful of independents. Networks made a fortune because they were the only game in town. Now there are dozens—and, in some areas, hundreds—of TV channels to choose from.

The final episode of *Seinfeld* made media headlines. Yet thirty years ago *Seinfeld*'s ratings wouldn't have made Nielsen's list of top twenty-five shows of the season. With an almost infinite number of options, the chances of a broadcast, even a network broadcast, reaching almost everyone are close to zero.

Even worse is the World Wide Web. At last count there were nearly two million different commercial Web sites. That means there are about twenty-five people online for every single Web site . . . hardly a mass market of interest to an Interruption Marketer.

AltaVista, one of the most complete and most visited search engines on the Internet, claims to have indexed 100 million pages. That means their computer has surfed and scanned 100 million pages of information, and if you do a search, that's the database you're searching through.

It turns out that in response to people who do searches online, AltaVista delivers about 900 million pages a month. That means the average page that they have indexed in their search engine is called up exactly *nine* times a month. Imagine that. Millions of dollars invested in building snazzy corporate marketing sites and an average of nine people a month search for and find any given page of information on this search engine.

This is a very, very big haystack, and Interruption Marketers don't have that many needles.

Marketers have invested (and almost completely wasted) more than a billion dollars on Web sites as a way of cutting through the clutter. General Electric has a site with thousands of pages. Ziff-Davis offers a site with more than 250,000 pages! And a direct result of this attempt to cut through the clutter is the most cluttered, least effective marketing of all.

THE FOUR APPROACHES TO KEEPING MASS MARKETING ALIVE

A quick look at the newsstand at Barnes & Noble will confirm that the problem of clutter saturation isn't limited to electronic media. There are enough consumer magazines (ig-noring the even larger category of trade magazines for a mo-ment) to keep a reader busy reading magazines full-time, twenty-four hours a day, seven days a week.

Obviously the mass market is dying. The vast splintering of media means that a marketer can't reach a significant per-centage of the population with any single communication. That's one reason the Super Bowl can charge so much for ad-vertisements. Big events are unique in their ability to deliver about half the consumers watching TV, so they're the perfect platform for Interruption Marketing aimed at the mass audi-ence.

Other than buying even more traditional advertising, how are mass marketers dealing with this profound infoglut? They're taking four approaches:

1. First, they're spending more in odd places. Not just on traditional TV ads, but on a wide range of interesting and ob-scure media. Campbell's Soup bought ads on parking meters. Macy's spends a fortune on its parade. Kellogg's has spent millions building a presence on the World Wide Web—a fasci-nating way to sell cereal.

Companies have seen that a mass market broadcast strat-egy isn't working as well as it used to, especially when target-ing the hard-to-reach upper-income demographic. As this lucrative audience spends less time watching TV, marketers are working overtime trying to find media with less clutter, where their interruption techniques can be more effective.

Marketers hire Catalina Corporation to print their coupons on the back of receipts at the grocery store. They buy ads on the floor of the cereal aisle. There are ads atop taxis in New York City and on the boards around the rink at the hockey game. Fox even figured out a way to sell the rights to the small area over the catcher's shoulder, so TV viewers would see the ad throughout an entire baseball game.

2. The second technique is to make advertisements ever more controversial and entertaining. Coca-Cola hired talent agency CAA to enlist topflight Hollywood directors to make commercials. Candies features a woman sitting on a toilet in its magazine ads (for shoes!). Spike Lee's ad agency did more than $50 million in billings last year.

Of course, as the commercials try harder to get your attention, the clutter becomes even worse. An advertiser who manages to top a competitor for the moment has merely raised the bar. Their next ad will have to be even more outlandish in order to top the competition, not to mention their previous ad, to keep the consumer's attention.

The cost of making a first-rate TV commercial is actually far more, per minute, than that of producing a major Hollywood motion picture. Talking frogs, computer graphics, and intense editing now seem to be a requirement.

A side effect of the focus on entertainment is that it gives the marketer far less time to actually market. In a fifteen-second commercial (increasingly attractive as a cost-cutting way to interrupt people even more often), ten or even twelve seconds are devoted to getting your attention, while just a few heartbeats are reserved for the logo, the benefit, and the call to action.

Take the interruption challenge! Write down all the companies that ran commercials during your favorite TV show last night. Write down all the companies that paid good money to buy banners on the Web during your last surfing expedition. If you can list more than 10 percent of them, you're certainly the exception.

3. The third approach used to keep mass marketing alive is to change ad campaigns more often in order to keep them "interesting and fresh." Tony the Tiger and Charlie the Tuna and the Marlboro man are each worth billions of dollars in brand equity to the companies that built them. The marketers behind them have invested a fortune over the last forty years making them trusted spokesmen (or spokesanimals) for their brands.

Nike, on the other hand, just ran a series of ads without the swoosh, arguably one of the most effective logos of the last generation. Apple Computer changes its tag line annually. Wendy's and McDonald's and Burger King jump from one approach to the other, all hoping for a holy grail that captures attention.

In exchange for these brief bits of attention (remember the hoopla when they replaced Mikey on the Life box?) these marketers are trading in the benefits of a long-term brand recognition campaign. It's a trade they're willing to make, because Interruption Marketing requires it. Without attention, there is no ad.

4. The fourth and last approach, which is as profound as the other three, is that many marketers are abandoning advertising and replacing it with direct mail and promotions. Marketers now allocate about 52 percent of their annual ad budgets for direct mail and promotions, a significant increase over past years.

Of the more than $200 billion spent on consumer advertising last year in the United States, more than $100 billion was spent on direct mail campaigns, in-store promotions, coupons, freestanding inserts, and other nontraditional media. Last year alone Wunderman, Cato, Johnson did more than $1.6 billion in billings for its clients (folks like AT&T).

The next time you get a glossy mailing for a Lexus or enter an instant win sweepstakes at the liquor store, you're seeing the results of this trend toward increased direct marketing efforts. Advertisers are using them because they work. They are somewhat more effective at interrupting you than an ad. They're somewhat more measurable than a billboard. Best of all, they give the marketers another tool to use in their increasingly frustrating fight against clutter. After all, there are only five or ten pieces of junk mail in your mailbox every day—not 3,000. And another few feet of shelf space at the supermarket can lead to a dramatic upturn in sales.

Direct Marketing Breaks Through the Clutter, Temporarily

Even though they work better than advertising, these techniques are astonishingly wasteful. A 2 percent response for a direct mail campaign will earn the smart marketer a raise at most companies. But a 2 percent response means that the same campaign was trashed, ignored, or rejected by an amazing 98 percent of the target audience! From the perspective of the marketer, however, if the campaign earns more than it costs, it's worth doing again.

Of course, just as suburbanites learned when they fled the

city to avoid the crowds, if a strategy works, other people will be right on your heels. That bucolic countryside fills up rapidly with other people looking to get away from it all. Correspondingly, as each of these promotional media becomes measurably effective, every smart marketer rushes to join in. Finding a unique approach that cuts through the clutter is usually very short-lived.

Virtually every supermarket now charges a shelving allowance, for example, which manufacturers pay for if they want more shelf space for their products. Every liquor store is already jammed with promotions. Every mailbox in the country is brimming with catalogs for clothes, gardening equipment, and fountain pens.

Direct marketers are responding to this glut by using computers. With access to vast amounts of computerized customer information, marketers can collate and cross-reference a database of names to create a finely tuned mailing list and then send them highly targeted messages. For example, a direct marketer might discover that based on past results, the best prospects for its next campaign are single women who are registered Democrats, who make more than $58,000 a year, and who have no balance on their credit card. This information is easily available, and marketers are now racing to make their direct marketing ever more targeted.

Of course, database marketing is a weapon available to any marketer, so like all trends in Interruption Marketing, this one will soon lose its edge. When others jump in as well, the clutter will inevitably catch up.

The last frontier of Interruption Marketing appears to be exemplified by the movie *Titanic*. James Cameron showed the world that outspending any rational marketer will indeed cut through the clutter. Hollywood has jumped on this band-wagon with marketing campaigns for *Godzilla* and other films that at first glance can't possibly bring in enough ticket sales to justify the expense.

Nike uses the same approach to sell sneakers, and now this radical overspending strategy is being used by others, especially on the Internet. The thinking behind it is based on an all-or-nothing roll of the dice. Basically, because clutter is so pervasive, anyone who can successfully break through and create a new mass market product will reap huge rewards. And betting vast amounts of other people's money on that breakthrough is one way to play.

Of course, once there's a proven pattern that big spending can win, others in the category will jump in as well. The bar will be raised yet again, and the only winners will be the me-dia companies that sell the airtime and ad space in the first place.

WHY AD AGENCIES DON'T WORK TO SOLVE THE PROBLEM

What about the ad agencies? With so many talented people, why aren't they working to solve this problem?

Unfortunately the clutter wars are taking their casualties at the agency side as well. The big agencies, the ones that could afford to take the lead in this challenge, are faced with three dismal problems:

1. First, clients are giving the agencies a much shorter leash. Leo Burnett used to keep clients for twenty or thirty

years. Levi's stayed at FCB for sixty-eight years. That's so long that not one person at either company was probably born when the account work was started on Levi's.

Today, however, it's not unusual for a marketer to change agencies after two or three years. Companies that fired their ad agencies in the last year include Bank of America, Compaq, Goodyear, and many more.

2. The second problem is that the stock market has been conducive to agency consolidations. The best way to make money in advertising today is to buy ad agencies and take them public. As a result, some of the best minds in the business have been focusing on building agencies, not brands.

3. Last, the commission structure that every ad agency was built upon has been dramatically dismantled. Traditionally agencies were paid by media companies. They got to keep 15 percent of all the ad money the client spent on ad space in the form of a commission from the magazines and TV networks where they ran their ads. This meant that big clients could generate huge profits for the ad agencies, which funded work on new approaches to advertising as well as the innovative ads for new, smaller clients. But now the big guys have decided to put a stop to this subsidizing, and it's rare to find an ad agency that still gets a straight 15 percent commission on media buys for their big clients.

INTERRUPTION MARKETERS FACE A CATCH-22

To summarize the problem that faces the Interruption Marketer:

1. Human beings have a finite amount of attention.

You can't watch everything, remember everything, or do everything. As the amount of noise in your life increases, the percentage of messages that get through inevitably decreases.

2. Human beings have a finite amount of money.

You also can't buy everything. You have to choose. But because your attention is limited, you'll be able to choose only from those things you notice.

3. The more products offered, the less money there is to go around.

It's a zero sum game. Every time you buy a Coke, you don't buy a Pepsi. As the number of companies offering products increases, and as the number of products each company offers multiplies, it's inevitable that there will be more losers than winners.

4. In order to capture more attention and more money, Interruption Marketers must increase spending.

Spending less money than your competitors on advertising in a cluttered environment inevitably leads to decreased sales.

5. But this increase in marketing exposure costs big money.

Interruption Marketers have no choice but to spend a bigger and bigger portion of their company's budgets on breaking through the clutter.

6. But, as you've seen, spending more and more money in order to get bigger returns leads to ever more clutter.

7. Catch-22: The more they spend, the less it works. The less it works, the more they spend.

*   *   *

Is mass marketing due for a cataclysmic shakeout? Absolutely. A new form of marketing is changing the landscape, and it will affect Interruption Marketing as significantly as the automobile affected the makers of buggy whips.

TWO

Permission Marketing—The Way to Make Advertising Work Again

Powerful advertising is anticipated, personal, and relevant.

WHAT IF YOU COULD TURN CLUTTER into an asset? What if the tremendous barriers faced by Interruption Marketers actually became an *advantage* for you and your company? The truth is that even though clutter is bad and getting worse, Permission Marketers turn clutter to their advantage. In fact, the worse the clutter gets, the *more profitable* your Permission Marketing efforts become.

In this chapter I'm going to outline the core ideas behind Permission Marketing. Every marketing campaign gets better when an element of permission is added. In some cases, a switch to marketing with permission can fundamentally change a company's entire business model and profit structure. At the very least, the basic concepts of permission will help you formulate and launch every marketing campaign with greater insight and success.

Interruption Marketing fails because it is unable to get enough attention from consumers. Permission Marketing works by taking advantage of the same problem—there just isn't enough attention to go around.

We Are All Running Out of Time

Two hundred years ago natural resources and raw materials were scarce. People needed land to grow food, metal to turn into pots, and silicates and other natural elements to make windows for houses. Tycoons who cornered the market in these and other resources made a fortune. By making a market in a scarce resource, you can make a profit.

With the birth of the Industrial Revolution, and the growth of our consumer economy, the resource scarcity shifted from raw materials to finished goods. Factories were at capacity. The great industrialists, like Carnegie and Ford, earned their millions by providing what the economy demanded. Marketers could call the shots, because other options were scarce.

Once factories caught up with demand, marketers developed brands that consumers would desire and pay a premium to own. People were willing to walk a mile for a Camel, and they'd rather fight than switch their brand of cigarette. When brands were new and impressive, owning the right brand was vital.

But in today's free market there are plenty of factories, plenty of brands, and way too many choices. With just a little effort and a little savings we can get almost anything we want. You can find a TV set in every house in this country. People throw away their broken microwave ovens instead of having them repaired.

This surplus situation, or abundance of goods, is especially clear when it comes to information and services. Making another copy of a software program or printing another CD costs almost nothing. Bookstores compete to offer 50,000,

100,000, or even 1 million different books—each for less than $25. There's a huge surplus of intellectual property and services out there.

Imagine a tropical island populated by people with simple needs and plenty of resources. You won't find a bustling economy there. That's because you need two things in order to have an economy: people who want things, and a scarcity of things they want. Without scarcity, there's no basis for an economy.

When there's an abundance of any commodity, the value of that commodity plummets. If a commodity can be produced at will and costs little or nothing to create, it's not likely to be scarce, either. That's the situation with information and services today. They're abundant and cheap. Information on the Web, for example, is plentiful and free.

Software provides another example. The most popular Web server is not made by Microsoft or Netscape. And it doesn't cost $1,000 or $10,000. It's called Apache, and it's created by a loosely knit consortium of programmers, and it's totally free. Free to download, free to use. As resources go, information is not scarce.

There is one critical resource, though, that is in chronically short supply. Bill Gates has just as much as you do. And even Warren Buffet can't buy more. That scarce resource is *time*. And in light of today's information glut, that means there's a vast shortage of *attention*.

This combined shortage of time and attention is unique to today's information age. *Consumers are now willing to pay handsomely to save time, while marketers are eager to pay bundles to get attention.*

Interruption Marketing is the enemy of anyone trying to save time. By constantly interrupting what we are doing at any given moment, the marketer who interrupts us not only tends to fail at selling his product, but wastes our most coveted commodity, time. In the long run, therefore, Interruption Marketing is doomed as a mass marketing tool. The cost to the consumer is just too high.

The alternative is Permission Marketing, which offers the consumer an opportunity to *volunteer* to be marketed to. By talking only to volunteers, Permission Marketing guarantees that consumers pay more attention to the marketing message. It allows marketers to tell their story calmly and succinctly, without fear of being interrupted by competitors or Interruption Marketers. It serves both consumers and marketers in a symbiotic exchange.

Permission Marketing encourages consumers to participate in a long-term, interactive marketing campaign in which they are rewarded in some way for paying attention to increasingly relevant messages. Imagine your marketing message being read by 70 percent of the prospects you send it to (not 5 percent or even 1 percent). Then imagine that more than 35 percent respond. That's what happens when you interact with your prospects one at a time, with individual messages, exchanged with their permission over time.

Permission marketing is anticipated, personal, relevant.

Anticipated—people look forward to hearing from you.
Personal—the messages are directly related to the individual.
Relevant—the marketing is about something the prospect is
    interested in.

I know what you're thinking. There's a catch. If you have to personalize every customer message, that's prohibitive. If you're still thinking within the framework of traditional marketing, you're right. But in today's information age, targeting customers individually is not as difficult as it sounds. Permission Marketing takes the cost of interrupting the consumer and spreads it out, over not one message, but dozens of messages. And this leverage leads to substantial competitive advantages and profits. While your competition continues to interrupt strangers with mediocre results, your Permission Marketing campaign is turning strangers into friends and friends into customers.

The easiest way to contrast the Interruption Marketer with the Permission Marketer is with an analogy about getting married. It also serves to exemplify how sending multiple individualized messages over time works better than a single message, no matter how impressive that single message is.

The Two Ways to Get Married

The Interruption Marketer buys an extremely expensive suit. New shoes. Fashionable accessories. Then, working with the best database and marketing strategists, selects the demographically ideal singles bar.

Walking into the singles bar, the Interruption Marketer marches up to the nearest person and proposes marriage. If turned down, the Interruption Marketer repeats this process on every person in the bar.

If the Interruption Marketer comes up empty-handed after spending the entire evening proposing, it is obvious that the blame should be placed on the suit and the shoes. The tailor is fired. The strategy expert who picked the bar is fired. And the Interruption Marketer tries again at a different singles bar.

If this sounds familiar, it should. It's the way most large marketers look at the world. They hire an agency. They build fancy ads. They "research" the ideal place to run the ads. They interrupt people and hope that one in a hundred will go ahead and buy something. Then, when they fail, they fire their agency!

The other way to get married is a lot more fun, a lot more rational, and a lot more successful. It's called dating.

A Permission Marketer goes on a date. If it goes well, the two of them go on another date. And then another. Until, after ten or twelve dates, both sides can really communicate with each other about their needs and desires. After twenty dates they meet each other's families. Finally, after three or four months of dating, the Permission Marketer proposes marriage.

Permission Marketing is just like dating. It turns strangers into friends and friends into lifetime customers. Many of the rules of dating apply, and so do many of the benefits.

THE FIVE STEPS TO DATING YOUR CUSTOMER

Every marketer must offer the prospective customer an incentive for volunteering. In the vernacular of dating, that means you have to offer something that makes it interesting enough to go out on a first date. A first date, after all, represents a big investment in time, money, and ego. So there had better be reason enough to volunteer.

Without a selfish reason to continue dating, your new potential customer (and your new potential date) will refuse you a second chance. If you don't provide a benefit to the consumer for paying attention, your offer will suffer the same fate as every other ad campaign that's vying for their attention. It will be ignored.

The incentive you offer to the customer can range from information, to entertainment, to a sweepstakes, to outright payment for the prospect's attention. But the incentive must be overt, obvious, and clearly delivered.

This is the most obvious difference between Permission Marketing and Interruption Marketing. Interruption Marketers spend all their time interrupting strangers, in an almost pitiful attempt to bolster popularity and capture attention. Permission Marketers spend as little time and money talking to strangers as they can. Instead they move as quickly as they can to turn strangers into prospects who choose to "opt in" to a series of communications.

Second, using the attention offered by the consumer, the marketer offers a curriculum over time, teaching the consumer about the product or service he has to offer. The Permission Marketer knows that the first date is an opportunity to sell the other person on a second date. Every step along the way has to be interesting, useful, and relevant.

Since the prospect has agreed to pay attention, it's much easier to teach him about your product. Instead of filling each ensuing message with entertainment designed to attract attention or with sizzle designed to attract the attention of strangers, the Permission Marketer is able to focus on product benefits—on specific, focused ways this product will help that prospect. Without question, this ability to talk freely over time is the most powerful element of this marketing approach.

The third step involves reinforcing the incentive. Over time, any incentive wears out. Just as your date may tire of even the finest restaurant, the prospective customer may show fatigue with the same repeated incentive. The Permission Marketer must work to reinforce the incentive, to be sure that the attention continues. This is surprisingly easy. Because this is a two-way dialogue, not a narcissistic monologue, the marketer can adjust the incentives being offered and fine-tune them for *each* prospect.

Along with reinforcing the incentive, the fourth step is to increase the level of permission the marketer receives from the potential customer. Now I won't go into detail on what step of the dating process this corresponds to, but in marketing terms, the goal is to motivate the consumer to give more and more permission over time. Permission to gather more data about the customer's personal life, or hobbies, or interests. Permission to offer a new category of product for the customer's consideration. Permission to provide a product sample. The range of permission you can obtain from a customer is very wide and limited only by its relevance to the customer.

Over time, the marketer uses the permission he's obtained to change consumer behavior—that is, get them to say "I do." That's how you turn permission into profits. After permission is granted, that's how it becomes a truly significant asset for the marketer. Now you can live happily ever after by repeating the aforementioned process while selling your customer more and more products. In other words, the fifth and final step is to leverage your permission into a profitable situation for both of you. Remember, you have access to the most valuable thing a customer can offer—attention.

Five Steps to Dating Your Customer

1. Offer the prospect an incentive to volunteer.
2. Using the attention offered by the prospect, offer a curriculum over time, teaching the consumer about your product or service.
3. Reinforce the incentive to guarantee that the prospect maintains the permission.
4. Offer additional incentives to get even more permission from the consumer.
5. Over time, leverage the permission to change consumer behavior toward profits.

PERMISSION IS AN INVESTMENT

Nothing good is free, and that goes double for permission. Acquiring solid, deep permission from targeted customers is an investment.

What is one permission worth? According to their annual report, AOL has paid as much as $300 to get one new customer. American Express invests nearly $150 to get a new cardholder. Does American Express earn enough in fees to justify this expense? Not at all. But the other benefits associated with acquiring the permission to market to a card member outweigh the high cost. Amex sells its customers a wide range of products, not just an American Express card. They also use sophisticated database management tools to track customer behavior so they can tailor offers to individuals. They leverage their permission to increase revenue.

One of the leading brokerage houses on Wall Street is currently paying $15 in media acquisition costs just for permission to call a potential customer on the phone! Yes, it's that expensive, and yes, it's worth even more than that. They've discovered that the yield from an anticipated, welcomed, personal phone call is so much higher than a cold call during dinner that they're willing to pay handsomely for the privilege.

While these (and other) marketers have discovered the power of permission, many Interruption Marketers have found, to their chagrin, that the cost of generating one new customer is rapidly approaching the net present value of that consumer. In other words, they're close to losing money on every customer, so they try to make it up in volume.

Permission Marketing cuts through the clutter and allows a marketer to speak to prospects as friends, not strangers. This personalized, anticipated, frequent, and relevant communication has infinitely more impact than a random message displayed in a random place at a random moment.

Permission Marketing Is Anticipated, Personal, Relevant

Anticipated—people look forward to hearing from you.
Personal—the messages are directly related to the individual.
Relevant—the marketing is about something the prospect is interested in.

Think about choosing a nice restaurant for dinner. If you learn about a restaurant from a cold-calling telemarketer or from an unsolicited direct mail piece, you're likely to ignore the recommendation. But if a trusted friend offers a restaurant recommendation, you're likely to try it out.

Permission Marketing lets you turn strangers, folks who might otherwise ignore your unsolicited offer, into people willing to pay attention when your message arrives in an expected, appreciated way.

An Interruption Marketer looks for a job by sending a résumé to one thousand strangers. A Permission Marketer gets a job by focusing on one company and networking with it, consulting for it, and working with it until the company trusts him enough to offer him a full-time position.

A book publisher that uses Interruption Marketing sells children's books by shipping them to bookstores, hoping that the right audience will stumble across them. A Permission Marketer builds book clubs at every school in the country.

An Interruption Marketer sells a new product by introducing it on national TV. A Permission Marketer sells a new product by informing all her existing customers about a way to get a free sample.

	Interruption	Permission
Anticipated	No	Yes
Personal	Not usually	Yes
Relevant	Sometimes	Yes

PERMISSION MARKETING IS AN OLD CONCEPT WITH NEW RELEVANCE

Permission Marketing isn't as glamorous as hiring Steven Spielberg to direct a commercial starring a bevy of supermodels. It isn't as easy as running an ad a few more times. It isn't as cheap as building a Web site and hoping that people find it on a search engine. In fact, it's hard work.

Worst of all, Permission Marketing requires patience. Permission Marketing campaigns grow over time—the opposite of what most marketers look for these days. And Permission Marketing requires a leap of faith. Even a bad interruption campaign gets some results right away, while a permission campaign requires infrastructure and a belief in the durability of the permission concept before it blossoms with success.

But unlike Interruption Marketing, Permission Marketing is a measurable process. It evolves over time for every company that uses it. It becomes an increasingly valuable asset. The more you commit to Permission Marketing campaigns, the better they work over time. And these fast-moving, leveragable processes are the key to success in our cluttered age.

So if Permission Marketing is so effective, and the ideas behind it not really new, why was the concept not used with effectiveness years ago? Why was this book just published?

Permission Marketing has been around forever (or at least as long as dating), but it takes advantage of new technology better than other forms of marketing. The Internet is the greatest direct mail medium of all time, and the low cost of frequent interaction makes it ideal for Permission Marketing.

Originally, the Internet captured the attention of Interruption Marketers. They rushed in, spent billions of dollars applying their Interruption Marketing techniques, and discovered almost total failure. Permission Marketing is the tool that unlocks the power of the Internet. The leverage it brings to this new medium, combined with the pervasive clutter that infects the Internet and virtually every other medium, makes Permission Marketing the most powerful trend in marketing for the next decade.

As new forms of media develop and clutter becomes ever more intense, it's the asset of permission that will generate profits for marketers.

THREE

The Evolution of Mass Advertising

Mass advertising created mass marketers.

ONE HUNDRED YEARS AGO small companies ruled the earth. Virtually every retail dollar went to a small, individually owned business. Local businesses were responsive, trusted, and capable. They had the infrastructure to deal with clients who didn't have credit cards, telephones, or Federal Express account numbers.

Without a mass communication infrastructure or the technology to expand, businesses stayed small and local. It was impossible for them to imagine a nationwide advertising campaign. New customers were acquired one at a time, usually by word of mouth or by door-to-door canvassing.

Companies knew exactly what a new client was worth, and they acted accordingly. A proprietor would spend hours with a prospect, knowing that the individual interaction would pay off many times over.

Consumers responded to this personal care and developed the expectation that they would be sold to personally. The local bookseller would read a book before recommending it. The local cheese merchant would happily offer a taste of a new flavor to a customer. It wasn't unusual for a shopkeeper to spend some extra time with a customer, old or new, or for the merchant's supplier to also be his neighbor.

GIANT BRANDS GAVE RISE TO INTERRUPTIBLE MEDIA

Giant brands and multinational companies were created as the result of several interconnected sociotechnological changes that occurred simultaneously.

The first change was the Industrial Revolution. Without the economies of scale that came from building factories, there was no reason at all to get big. When everything was handmade, having more craftsmen didn't make your business more efficient or lucrative.

Once there were economies, though, businesses faced a choice. They could grow or they could wither. Many entrepreneurs saw the opportunity that came from scaling their businesses and raised the money to do just that.

Second, the development of the car and the truck made it possible to deliver things that were made more than a few miles away. Suddenly companies could buy things in bulk, manufacture many items, and then ship them around the country and even around the world.

As a result of these investments, companies needed mass advertising. It did no good to build a factory that was efficient at mass production if it was impossible to deliver those goods to a larger market. And you couldn't do that if you couldn't persuade consumers to buy them. Instead of relying solely on word of mouth and personalized sales, big companies had no choice but to discover a way to get lots and lots of people to buy the output of their factories.

The big surprise is that it wasn't factories or the car that caused the big increase in corporate profitability. It was advertising. The economies that came from establishing a product as the leading brand, the huge premiums that were derived by charging extra for a trusted name, dwarfed the savings in production.

Marketing rapidly became the most profitable part of the enterprise. In the words of one pundit, "Everything else is an expense." The ability to attract large numbers of customers with advertising was a revelation to these new companies. First enamored and then addicted, they based their entire business model and organization around the ability to reach the masses.

In the 1920s advertising men were considered the saviors of industrialized society, the sophisticated men who would harness the awesome power of the crowd to uplift society. Advertising was credited with bringing the clean, the pure, and the powerful to ordinary citizens, lowering prices, and vastly increasing the direct responsibility that manufacturers had over their products.

Once manufacturers began to advertise, they discovered (some quite by accident) an extraordinary truth: The more they advertised, the more sales they gained. And the value of the sales exceeded the cost of the advertising! The perpetual motion machine of commerce had arrived.

The development of content-filled media to hold all this advertising was a direct consequence of this discovery. Interruption Marketers needed something to interrupt, so newspapers flourished and magazines were started by the thousands. Did Interruption Marketing lead to the creation of mass media as we know it? Absolutely!

This evolution is best summarized by the story of Crisco.

CRISCO: PRODUCT-DRIVEN MARKETING EVOLUTION

In 1900 the folks at Procter & Gamble were heady with the success of Ivory soap. Ivory was the first packaged, branded soap that was able to compete with handmade soap or unpackaged, bulk soap from the local general store. It was an insanely profitable, fast-growing business for this young company, but Ivory's success quickly brought about a problem. There was a limited supply of cottonseed oil, a major ingredient in the manufacture of Ivory.

Cottonseed oil was produced by just a few tightly controlled trusts, and three huge vendors were able to purchase virtually all of the oil on the market. P&G desperately needed another product that would use lots of cottonseed oil. With two major products and an even greater need for cottonseed oil, P&G would garner more clout with the tightly held trusts. Greater clout would lead to more reliable supplies and better pricing for P&G.

For four years researchers worked to create the ideal product that would use a lot of cottonseed oil. Eventually they created Crisco, a product designed to replace lard just as Ivory had replaced homemade soap.

In 1908, when P&G introduced Crisco, there was no *Time* magazine, and no *General Hospital* on which to advertise. Without reliable mass media, P&G relied on Permission Marketing.

They started by paying the train lines (the equivalent of today's airlines) to use Crisco instead of lard in the pies they served on board (and to inform their customers when it was served). They secured testimonials from doctors and even rabbis, one of whom said that Crisco was "the greatest advance for Judaism in four thousand years."

P&G held society teas in all the major cities, asking a prominent citizen to invite the leading ladies to attend. Of course, everything offered to go with the tea was baked with Crisco.

Finally, P&G introduced a series of free cookbooks. In a classic Permission Marketing technique, P&G didn't try to sell the product. Instead they promoted the free cookbook. Once a prospect raised her hand for this information, the stories inside the cookbook taught her about the benefits of the product. The book quickly became a "best-seller."

The campaign succeeded. Crisco rapidly became a major profit center for P&G. It also impacted grocery stores and changed the way people cooked.

But once the ball began rolling, Crisco realized that Permission Marketing alone couldn't expand the brand's popularity fast enough. So they took advantage of the lack of clutter and switched gears to an Interruption Marketing campaign. Now that they had a sales base, they wanted to expand it, fast. So they began buying advertising anywhere they could find it. And because there was so little clutter, the advertising popularized the brand quickly and cheaply.

How Interruption Marketing Creates Permission Opportunities

Once the corporate world caught a glimpse of mass brand advertising, mass marketers were hooked on Interruption Marketing. The reasons were simple:

- Interruption Marketing was easy. Build a few ads, run them everywhere.
- Interruption Marketing was scalable. If you need more sales, buy more ads.
- Interruption Marketing was predictable. With experience, a mass marketer could tell how many dollars in revenue one more dollar in ad spending would generate.
- Interruption Marketing fit the command and control bias of big companies. It was totally controlled by the advertiser, with no weird side effects.
- Interruption Marketing was profitable. The right product generated more profit than it cost the company to advertise.

Mass marketers optimized their organizations for this approach. They created brand managers and advertising agencies and measurement companies and focus groups and myriad other techniques to institutionalize their attachment to Interruption Marketing.

This focus on Interruption Marketing allowed the big brands to become even bigger and more dominant. The top one hundred advertisers account for more than 87 percent of all advertising expenditures in this country. And more than eighty of these companies have been advertising for more than twenty years.

This has two important implications. First, behavior by these top advertisers dictates and drives the market as a whole. Second, and more important, is the fact that there are virtually no first-generation marketers working at these companies.

To put it bluntly, big companies don't hire people to reinvent their already successful marketing techniques. Instead they hire and train people to do exactly what the last advertising people did. They market Crisco the same way they did eighty years ago. The Rice Krispies box hasn't changed in years. Ford uses a marketing and distribution network it built in 1920.

Second- and third-generation marketers don't want to rock the boat in which they're sailing. They may have noticed that their current marketing techniques don't seem to work as well as they used to, but they weren't hired to demolish the distribution channel or to question the very foundation of their marketing heritage.

Permission Marketing represents a huge threat as well as a huge opportunity. Just as the fax machine altered the landscape of courier services and Federal Express, Permission Marketing will change the way companies market products.

Many of the big companies will stick to their knitting and remain faithful to the marketing methods that got them where they are today. This creates mammoth opportunities for new companies, for companies with nothing to lose, for companies with the flexibility and initiative to try a very different way of gaining and keeping customers.

FOUR

Getting Started—Focus on Share of Customer, Not Market Share

Fire 70 percent of your customers and watch your profits go up!

FIVE YEARS AGO Don Peppers and Martha Rogers wrote a book that changed the marketing landscape forever. Titled *The One to One Future*, it proposed a radical rethinking of the way marketers treat their customers. Peppers and Rogers presented a manifesto for how companies can increase their profits by selling more things to fewer customers. In other words, they believe it's wiser to focus more on increasing sales to a smaller percentage of your existing customers than to find new ones.

The thinking behind their book is straightforward, and it led directly to the agenda behind Permission Marketing: Getting a new customer is expensive. It takes money to get his attention, and it takes continuing effort to educate him (Interruption Marketing is expensive, and so is the process of winning a customer's trust). It's also expensive for the customer, who has to spend time evaluating and learning about the features and benefits of a product.

So, argue the authors, instead of focusing on how to maximize the number of new customers, the focus should be on keeping customers longer and getting far more money from each of them over time.

It's back to the old days, when merchants had a limited supply of customers and worked to get the maximum revenue from each one. Except now, with technology, companies can combine this Old World thinking with the ability to dramatically grow their customer base at the same time.

If AT&T spends hundreds of dollars to get a new long-distance customer, and that customer pays just $20 per month for AT&T's services, then they have to be figuring out other ways to generate revenue through their interaction with *that* customer, not spending all their energy getting yet another new customer.

By selling cellular phone services, home security services, and an increasing array of other items, AT&T can recoup the expense of obtaining these customers.

Levi's has built one of the single largest brands of women's jeans in the country. And they've done so without having any jeans in the store.

Instead women have their measurements taken by a trained specialist, who sends them to a computerized factory. There, a semicustom pair of jeans is made to order.

The shopper gets custom fit for a fraction of the cost. Levi's has a huge savings in inventory risk and advertising costs. Best of all, once a customer has given her measurements to Levi's, once she's endured the hassle of all that measurement taking, once she's worn a pair of custom jeans, would she even consider switching brands to save a few dollars?

To elaborate a little more on the one-to-one marketing

approach, Peppers and Rogers would like you to focus on four things when selling to customers:

1. Increase your "share of wallet." Figure out which needs you can satisfy, then use the knowledge you have, and the trust you've built, to make that additional sale.
2. Increase the durability of customer relationships. Invest money in customer retention, because it's a small fraction of the cost of customer acquisition.
3. Increase your product offerings to customers. By being customer-focused instead of retail-focused, or factory-focused, a manufacturer or merchant can widely increase its offerings, thus increasing share of wallet.
4. Create an interactive relationship that leads to meeting more customer needs. It's a cycle. By constantly encouraging the consumer to give more information, the marketer can offer more products.

This series of techniques isn't easy, nor is it free. If it was, everyone would do it. It requires a huge investment in scalable technology, along with the focus and commitment to do it right. It puts a lot more pressure on your organization as well, because as each customer becomes worth more, the cost of losing one increases.

USE PERMISSION EARLY IN THE MARKETING PROCESS

Don Peppers and Martha Rogers opened the eyes of many marketers and got them to look downstream after the first sale was made. By recognizing the huge cost of getting a first sale and the very high lifetime value of a customer, the one-to-one philosophy can dramatically increase profitability.

Permission Marketing demands that in addition to looking downstream, marketers now look upstream. The challenge facing most companies is that they notice people too late.

The process of getting new customers needs to be reengineered. Like caterpillars turning into butterflies, prospects go through a five-step cycle:

Strangers
Friends
Customers
Loyal Customers
Former Customers

Today, most marketers don't notice, track, or interact with people until they are customers. Some don't even pay close attention until the consumer becomes a loyal customer. Unfortunately, a few don't notice their customers until they become disgruntled *former* customers.

It's essential, given the high cost of talking to strangers, that marketers move their focus of attention up the stream. They need to have a process in place that nurtures total strangers from the moment they first indicate an interest.

At that moment, a suite of marketing messages must begin to be applied. The goal is to teach, cajole, and encourage this stranger to become a friend. And once she becomes a friend, to apply enough focused marketing to create a customer.

Do you know how your company does this now? Most marketers have no idea. They rely on a hodgepodge of randomly delivered interruptions and hope that from this primordial soup will rise a fully formed customer.

Computers and Permission Marketing can change that. You can now choose *whom* you reach. *When* you reach them. The order of the messages. The benefits offered. You can create dozens or even hundreds of paths for an individual to follow from the first contact until the highest level of permission is granted.

If the marketing messages you send are anticipated, relevant, and personal, they will cut through the clutter and increase the prospect's knowledge of the benefits you offer. An organization that is focused on this process early on will always outperform one that isn't.

THE NATURAL SYNERGY OF PERMISSION AND ONE-TO-ONE MARKETING

As you've seen, Permission Marketing is the cousin of one-to-one marketing. Where Peppers and Rogers begin the process with the first sale, permission begins the process with the very first contact.

Permission Marketing works to turn strangers into friends and then friends into customers. One-to-one marketing uses the very same techniques, incorporating knowledge, frequency, and relevance to turn customers into supercustomers. One-to-one doesn't compete with Permission Marketing; it's part of the very same continuum. The one-to-one marketer takes the permission that's been granted after someone be-

comes a customer and uses that permission to create even better customers. The better the permission, the more profit created.

> The one-to-one marketer works to change his focus from finding
> as many new customers as he can to extracting the maximum
> value from each customer.
>
> The Permission Marketer works to change his focus from
> finding as many prospects as he can to converting the largest
> number of prospects into customers. Then he leverages the
> permission on an ongoing basis.

You can't build a one-to-one relationship with a customer
unless the customer explicitly agrees to the process. Everything from discovering a shoe size to building mutually dependent computer systems with a major vendor requires an
overt agreement from both sides.

By measuring the depth of permission you have with each
customer (one may allow you to send merchandise "on approval," another may let you call them when a new product
comes in), you can begin to track the benefits of your investment in Permission Marketing. By focusing on how deep your
permission is with your existing customers, you can begin to
recognize the value of your permission asset.

Frank Britt and Tim DeMello run a company called
Streamline that is at the vanguard of the junction between
Permission Marketing and one-to-one marketing. Streamline
capitalizes on the technologies and social shifts that are
changing our lives, and they are building a fantastic business
that serves as a model for the future. They offer to save cus-

tomers hours and hours of time each week by doing virtually all of their routine errands.

A call to Streamline leads to a customized sales pitch by a trained Streamline sales rep. And in a surprisingly high number of cases, that sales pitch leads to a first sale. Then Streamline comes to your house and installs a large wooden box and a refrigerator in your garage. Next they ask to come into your house so that they can scan the UPC codes on every item in your fridge and food cabinet. They take down the name of your pharmacy and where you like your clothes dry-cleaned. Talk about permission!

Then, using the Web, you log on each week and tell Streamline what you need. You fill out a preautomated shopping list. They pick up dry cleaning and prescriptions and photos as well. Then, while you're at work, they do all your errands, pick up what you need, and drop it off at your house.

Streamline does this for about $30 a month. And the more services they offer, the more permission they get from customers. In a single year the average customer places forty-seven orders and spends more than $5,000 with them. Multiply that by millions of potential customers and you see the size of the opportunity! As the company gains more permission, it's not hard to imagine them branching into house-cleaning, housepainting, gardening, and a huge range of home care and home delivery services.

By "owning" permission to market new services, and by using one-to-one techniques to know and remember your preferences, Streamline is creating a megabusiness for the next century. They're building an asset that has nothing to do with brand and everything to do with their relationship with you.

Will Streamline find competition? Without a doubt. But once they've established permission with their customers, it will be extremely difficult for a competitor to dislodge them.

A more familiar example is Amazon.com. Ask most sentient humans and they'll tell you Amazon is a bookstore on the Web. Analysts will tell you that they're one of the biggest Internet-first brands.

Yet if Amazon is determined to be a bookseller, they've got big troubles. First, they pay far more for books than Barnes & Noble because of their smaller scale. But even if they overcome that disadvantage, other online sellers, like the new online service from Bertelsmann (the largest publisher of books in the world), will doubtless be able to compete on price.

So why is Amazon so busy building its customer base, losing money on each customer, and trying to make it up in volume? Why does their prospectus claim that they're losing money and see no end in sight for the losses?

Amazon appears to be building a permission asset, not a brand asset. Amazon has overt permission to track which books you buy and which books you browse. They have explicit permission to send you promotional e-mail messages. They are building special-interest communities in which Amazon and its customers will be able to talk with each other about specific genres of books. Why? Where's the payoff?

The payoff comes the day Amazon decides to publish books. This is where the profit lies and where Amazon is best able to leverage their permission asset.

A book costs about $2 to print and $20 in the store. A huge gulf! But most of that money disappears in advertising, shipping, and especially in the shredding of unsold books. What if you could remove all of those?

Imagine that Amazon.com sends a note to each of the one million people who bought a mystery novel from their site last year. (It costs them nothing to do that, of course, since e-mail is free.) In the note they ask if you'd like to buy the next Robert B. Parker novel, a Spenser mystery, which will be available exclusively from Amazon. And let's say a third of those customers respond and say, "Sure."

Now, Amazon can make the following extraordinary offer to Robert B. Parker. "Write the book. We'll edit it and typeset it and ship it directly to the 333,000 people who have preordered it. We'll deduct our costs and still have $1 million left over to pay you."

That's a lot of money for a mystery novel. Yet Amazon still will earn more than $4 million in profit from just one book.

Multiply that scenario by one hundred or one thousand books a year. Using permission, Amazon can fundamentally reconfigure the entire book industry, disintermediating and combining every step of the chain until there are only two: the writer and Amazon.

That's the way to visualize the power of permission. Technology enables marketers to have a perfect memory and provides them with the ability to customize correspondence on the fly and deliver it for free via e-mail. Combine that with a database of customers who expect to receive marketing messages from you because they gave you their permission, and most industry book chains should begin to see a looming threat.

By moving strangers up the permission ladder, from that very first interruption until the moment when the consumer gives you the permission to actually purchase products on their behalf, marketers are able to optimize their entire marketing process. The results can be fantastic. By dramatically increasing the measurability and efficiency of your marketing system, your company can multiply its profits.

> Traditional sales and marketing involves increasing market share, which means selling as much of your product as you can to as many customers as possible. One-to-one marketing involves driving for share of customer, which means ensuring that each individual customer who buys your product buys more product, buys only your brand, and is happy using your product instead of another to solve his problem. The true, current value of any one customer is a function of the customer's future purchases, across all the product lines, brands, and services offered by you.

How Firing 70 Percent of Your Customers Might Help Your Business

When you have a constant stream of strangers walking through the door as a result of Interruption Marketing, you don't have to worry as much about protecting your existing customers. Even though it's more profitable to cater to those existing customers, many marketers are uncomfortable with the shift in power it portends.

An online e-commerce story makes that lesson very clear. A consumer ordered several items from a small merchant selling CDs online. The consumer's credit card was quickly charged, but after three weeks nothing had arrived.

The consumer sent a polite note to the customer service e-mail address. No response. Another note. No response. So, after four weeks, the consumer wrote to the president of the company.

He wrote back the next day. His note consisted of just three words: "Get a life."

Did he burn a customer? Of course. That was his intention. But what he hasn't learned yet (and soon will, or he'll be gone) is that the act of dismissing that customer didn't cost him just one sale. It cost him the loss of permission to sell products to this woman for the rest of her life.

Think about it. He had her in a dialogue. He had her credit card number. He knows what CDs she likes. If he had treated that permission with respect, it could have easily led to $1,000 or $5,000 worth of CD sales over the lifetime of the relationship. But because the merchant was a physical retailer, accustomed to the anonymity and unpredictability of walk-in trade, he figured he was losing a $10 sale. Big mistake.

Compare this with the true story of a similar customer at a similar merchant, also online. This time, the complaint about slow delivery ended when it reached the customer service desk. The customer got a response within five minutes. The response was factual (the CD was misaddressed and had been returned), but the letter was apologetic. *And* the e-mail announced that to make up for the inconvenience, another CD by the same artist was going to be sent along for free.

Which merchant is most likely to earn a few thousand more dollars in incremental business due to the level of permission earned? Customer service has always mattered. But now that power has shifted to the consumer, it matters a great deal more.

Based on these stories, however, there's no way to know what type of customer, or future revenues, she represented. But given our vastly improved ability to "know" customers at an individual level, it's important to recognize that some customers carry a negative value, and it's sometimes wise to get rid of them. The reward comes to the marketer in the form of an increased ability to concentrate on nurturing the customers who represent the quality permission candidates for future business.

This means that sometimes you have to endure the entrepreneur's nightmare—you must fire a customer. In view of optimizing customer service, sometimes that's what it takes. A customer who distracts you, or one who cherry picks your line of products, or one who requires a disproportionate percentage of your company's time and resources, for example, is going to cost you money. Of course it matters how you fire a customer, too, and telling a customer with a valid complaint to "get a life" obviously falls short of wisdom.

Start by Getting the Customer to Raise His Hand

Not surprisingly, the first question most Interruption Marketers ask when they hear about Permission Marketing is, "How do you get people to sign up?" Because they were trained in the art of getting momentary reactions from large numbers of people, this part of the process is the most familiar to them.

Permission Marketing almost always follows the same simple steps. Each campaign is very different, but the concepts behind each step remain the same. Simply stated, you interrupt customers with a message designed to get them to raise their hand. That's the way they volunteer or say "yes" to begin a rewarding exchange of information accomplished over time, which builds trust that you can leverage into a sales relationship. But the first step is still to interrupt the consumer. That's one reason there will always be socially acceptable Interruption Marketing media. We need to get that initial attention.

Sometimes you're lucky enough that a stranger comes to you of his own accord. There will always be a few people who straggle onto your Web site, for example, or potential customers who call your toll-free number or walk into your store. These are the freebies. Most of the time, however, you've got to use the tried-and-true interruptive techniques to reach large numbers of people. Using measurable techniques, marketers can choose television, radio, print, direct mail, or electronic media to grab the attention of consumers. But without some way to grab the attention of a stranger, the permission process never starts.

Joanne Kates is the third-generation owner of Camp Arowhon, the oldest coed summer camp in North America. With a seventy-year history, great word of mouth, and a solid backlist, acquiring new customers is not her highest priority. Nonetheless, Arowhon needs a process to turn strangers into campers.

The camp uses Permission Marketing to accomplish this. The first step is to advertise at camp fairs and in magazines that feature groups of ads from summer camps. But unlike virtually all her competitors, Joanne isn't trying to sell her camp. She knows that no one chooses a summer camp for their children on the basis of a two-inch-square black-and-white advertisement.

Instead, her only goal in the ad, and at the trade show, is to get permission to send a video and a brochure. The ad sells the brochure, not the camp. Call the camp's number, and her staff will immediately qualify your interest and then send a video (perhaps the best-produced camp video in the market) and the brochure (also extremely well done).

The only goal of the video is to get permission to have a personal meeting. It doesn't sell the camp. It sells the meeting.

Now, fully qualified, and having seen the testimonials, the photographs, the facilities, and the happy campers, the family is ready to be sold on the camp. And that's done in person.

Once a camper attends for a summer, odds are that he or she will stay for more summers and bring a brother or sister as well. Which makes the sale worth nearly $20,000. By using Permission Marketing, Arowhon is able to make these significant step-by-step sales, with a very high efficiency.

At each step, the only goal of the next step is to expand permission. She interrupts to get permission to send a video using a small print ad, she uses the video to get permission to visit, she uses the visit to get permission to sell one summer, and she uses the summer to sell six more.

By focusing media on getting permission instead of making the ultimate sale, marketers are able to get far more out of their expenditures. The response rate to a free sample or an affinity program or a birthday club might be five or ten times the response rate of an ad asking for a sale.

This is a critical distinction. Step two in the process, after the consumer has been interrupted, is to make an offer and ask for volunteers. The offer should provide selfish motivation and offer virtually no downside.

An interrupted consumer is in no hurry to send you money or promise to invest a lot of time. An interrupted consumer won't fill out a long demographic form or get in his car to drive down to your automall. The less you ask of the consumer and the bigger the "bribe," the more likely the consumer will give you permission. The permission won't be broad or deep. But it will guarantee that your next interaction will be significantly more impactful.

When Hooked on Phonics ran nationwide radio advertising that helped them grow from zero to $100 million in revenue, they didn't try to sell anything on the radio. They didn't even mention the price. They sold the benefits by asking potential customers to call (800) ABCDEFG and get free information on how to help your kids. Free information. Help your kids. No downside. No money. This offer enticed millions of concerned parents to give permission to learn more about the product.

Hooked on Phonics gets far more attention from a completely qualified audience by using this two-step approach. Imagine how much harder it would have been for them to generate the same level of sales if they had tried to make the sale on the radio.

In order to make the marketing messages you send relevant and personal, you need to get some data. Permission Marketers are totally obvious about their objectives with the consumer. They make it crystal clear what they will be doing with the data they collect and exactly why it's beneficial to the consumer to give this data.

Consumers who visit a Web site are sometimes asked to give their phone number. But what's in it for the consumer? Without a specific reason for the consumer to behave, without a reward or a benefit, the overwhelmed consumer will refuse.

The reward you offer a consumer must be obvious and simple. To dramatize the importance of this stage, to make it crasser than it needs to be, I call it bait. No one would argue with the idea that when you go fishing, you ought to use the most effective, most obvious bait you can find. The same is true when you try to attract consumers.

After you've interrupted, engaged in a bargain, and exchanged data with the consumer, you need to teach and eventually leverage the permission you've obtained.

If you're in a medium where frequency is cheap (like the Net), take your time. Build trust through frequency. Tell your story patiently to each consumer who is willing to participate in the exchange.

Be personal. Be relevant. Be specific. And always be anticipated. Anticipation, of course, is even better than expectation. Without surprising the consumer, gradually raise the level of permission you extract.

Then, by constantly raising the magnitude of rewards you offer the prospect, you can fight attrition and compression and keep the consumer interested (compression is the tendency of rewards to become less effective with repetition). By continuing the dialogue, you can teach the consumer until a stranger becomes a friend and then a friend becomes a customer.

Of course, the process doesn't end with the first sale. It just becomes one-to-one marketing. Using the permission already granted, you then work hard to expand the share of wallet and build a permission asset that is ever deeper and more powerful.

GETTING THE CUSTOMERS TO RAISE THEIR HANDS TAKES PLANNING AND CAPITAL

Interrupting strangers and getting their attention in the first place is the glamorous part of marketing. Marketers and their advertising agencies live and die by the sizzle they create. They invest millions of dollars in a one-minute commercial, just to maximize the effectiveness of the execution.

A copywriter can make his career with a clever ad. In fact, a thirty-year-old clever campaign for the Volkswagen came back from the dead to generate millions of dollars in new Beetle sales for VW in 1998.

At the same time that Interruption Marketers are arming themselves with these killer executions, they're backing them with huge media budgets—media budgets that often dwarf the cost of inventing or even manufacturing the product in the first place.

All of this time and money is spent with one goal in mind: Interrupt people. If they remember the interruption the next day, even better. An Interruption Marketer who does a good job and boosts his direct mail response rate a tenth of a percent, or boosts morning-after recall a bit, is a hero. The entire point of the ad is to do that.

Wouldn't it be great if we could eliminate this incredibly wasteful part of the process? Unfortunately Permission Marketers cannot ignore the interruption part of the process. They can't walk away from the cost of getting strangers to raise their hands. But they *can* leverage the expense of that interruption across multiple interactions.

This is the big win here. By leveraging one interruption across numerous communications, the Permission Marketer has an unfair advantage. One message becomes six or ten or a hundred. A momentary interruption becomes a dialogue that can last for weeks or months.

Let's get specific and compare a marketer who had to make a single ad pay off with one who has the luxury of using permission. The Interruption Marketer must earn back the entire cost of the ad after just one viewing. So if it costs $2 to get one person to pay attention to the ad, it pays off only if, on average, it generates more than $2 in new business profits per viewing. If the impact is equal to or greater than the cost, go ahead and run the ad.

Running the same ad with frequency dramatically increases the amount of payback required. The marketer has to hope for $6 in new profits as a result of putting this ad in front of a prospect three times. If the third ad can't generate enough impact to make it worth running, it doesn't pay for itself.

Because frequency is free in an online permission program, and much more effective offline, the marketer has the luxury of riding the impact curve up without a matching cost curve. Once the initial toll is paid, in other words, the rest of the ride is close to free.

Thus, in this example, if that one interruption (which cost $2) can turn into five communications, the marketer gets a bonus of four extra chances to earn back that $2.

FIVE

How Frequency Builds Trust and Permission Facilitates Frequency

The unspoken secret that marketers are afraid to utter.

WHERE DOES trust come from?

This is what every marketer wants to know. Without trust, marketers know that there are no sales. Trust means the prospect believes not only that the product being sold will actually solve his problems, but that if for some reason it doesn't, the company will make good on its reputation of performance.

We happily pay a premium to buy our jewelry from a fancy store instead of from a shady character on the street. Why? Because we trust the store to sell us the real deal, while the guy with the watches in a briefcase represents a substantial risk.

Corporations pay consultants billions of dollars for their advice, when they could probably find similar advice down the street at the local community college. Why the premium? Because Bain and McKinsey and the like are trusted advisers. They've built enough of a track record, and enough confidence, that they can command a substantial premium.

Pan Am demonstrated the power of trust when it sold its

brand name a few years ago. An airline with no airplanes, no employees, no gates—not even any little packages of peanuts—sold its trusted name and logo for millions of dollars.

If trust is the objective, what are the tactics? How do some marketers manage to build trust while others are doomed to languish in obscurity?

Trust, it turns out, is not an event. You can't go from anonymity to trusted brand in a day. Instead it's a step-by-step process that requires time and money and commitment.

Before a marketer can build trust, it must breed familiarity. But there's no familiarity without awareness. And awareness—the science of letting people know you exist and getting them to understand your message—can't happen effectively in today's environment without advertising.

How to Turn Awareness into Familiarity

Since trust is the single biggest impediment to gaining new sales, and familiarity is the launching pad for trust, awareness is a critical issue.

If you don't care about the consequences, awareness isn't very difficult to generate. Run across the stage at the Oscars wearing nothing but socks and you're certain to generate some awareness. But it won't be the kind you can convert successfully into trust. Instead you'll need to use advertising to drive home your message.

But are there tactics and techniques that can make this process more efficient? Are all advertising campaigns created equal, or do some work better than others?

From an advertiser's point of view, the single most important tactic is frequency. Frequency is a simple concept: How
many times is your ad presented to a single individual? In
practice, though, frequency can create a number of pitfalls.

When advertising agencies measure their campaigns, they
look at reach and frequency. Reach is a fairly simple metric.
How many different people were exposed to each ad? Frequency, as we'll see in a moment, involves some more artful
measurements.

The first problem with frequency is that people may not
notice your ads no matter how frequently they're run. Morning-after recall of most TV campaigns varies, but it generally
falls below 10 percent. If the morning-after recall of your ad
comes in at 10 percent, that means your ad is considered successful even though almost ninety out of one hundred people
don't remember it.

Of the people who *do* notice your advertising, very few of
them focus on it, and fewer still may understand what you
were trying to say. Of course, you slaved over the script, cast
the commercial as if it were a major feature film, and edited
the piece into the middle of the night. But time-compressed,
info-cluttered consumers don't always get it.

And because a big part of every ad is a valiant attempt to
grab attention, the message isn't as pure as it could be. When
you've got animated tigers, dancing women, talking cars, and
Spike Lee directing, sometimes there isn't enough room to tell
your story.

To summarize, consumers may misunderstand the ad, ignore the ad, or forget the ad. So, like most advertising, nine
dollars out of every ten are wasted.

Direct response advertising is the most persuasive proof of this. Hire the best direct marketing firm in town, run a full-page in *The New York Times,* and count the orders that come in. If you're very good and pretty lucky, a few hundred (maybe a few thousand) people will read your ad. Fewer still will be persuaded enough by your deathless prose to trust you, will consider themselves failures unless they own your product, and will take action and actually send you money.

The response rate for ads like this is pitiful. This is the secret that marketers know—a single ad, no matter how well produced, no matter how compelling, is almost never enough to sell your product. To put this into positive terms: *Frequency works.*

Muhammad Ali did not become heavyweight champion of the world by punching twenty people one time each. No, he became the champ by punching one guy twenty times. By applying frequency to the poor opponent's head, Ali was able to bring his message home.

Advertising works the same way. Advertisers know that the single best way to make an advertising campaign work is to run the ads a lot. By all means, be sure to reach every possible consumer. But it's far more important to deliver advertising with frequency. Drill it home again and again.

The frequency you bring to an advertising campaign does two things. First, it cuts through the clutter with the sheer law of averages. If only 10 percent of the people remember your ad tomorrow, but your ad runs for thirty days in a row, sooner or later virtually everyone will remember it.

Second, frequency causes the consumer to focus on the message you're trying to get across. Just as repeating yourself to a four-year-old makes it more likely that he'll get the idea you're trying to communicate, just as repeating commands to a horse in training is more likely to change the horse's behavior, repeating yourself to a target consumer increases the odds that your message gets through.

Remember the first few times you heard a great pop song? You probably had a little trouble remembering the lyrics. It sure sounded as though Jimi Hendrix was saying, "Excuse me while I kiss this guy." Then, over time, as you heard the song over and over again, the message became more clear.

Remember the first time you saw Candice Bergen advertising Sprint, using a dime to make her point? That was a very confusing thirty seconds. Had Sprint just made pay phones cost a dime again? Was a dime more or less than you were paying now? Were there restrictions or special charges?

But after the third or fourth or tenth viewing, it probably became really clear that ten cents was a pretty good rate for a phone call, that Sprint offered it and AT&T didn't, and that if you called Sprint and switched, you could start saving money immediately. A pretty simple message, but it took a few times for it to sink in.

Moving on to a more complicated message (also in the phone business), how long did it take you to really understand what that whole "Friends and Family" campaign from MCI was all about? It's generally considered the single most effective ad campaign in the history of long-distance services, but it still took more than $100 million in advertising to drive the point home.

Nicholas Negroponte at the MIT Media Lab uses a great analogy to make a similar point: When you double the length of a fish, its weight goes up by a factor of four. The same thing is true for advertising. When you increase your frequency by 100 percent, you usually increase your effectiveness by 400 percent.

FREQUENCY AND TRUST OUTWEIGH REACH AND ITS GLAMOUR

So why does this seem to be such a big secret? Why do marketers fear frequency so much that they're often afraid to talk about it, afraid to hope for it?

Given the choice between reach and frequency, many unseasoned marketers make the mistake of going for reach instead. They argue that touching one hundred people with a brilliant ad is more effective than reaching twenty-five people four times each.

This approach seems encouraging, but research has shown it to be wrong. A simple true story takes the case to its extreme and demonstrates why reach alone can't build a brand, sell a product, or establish trust.

Years ago, a marketer with a new high-technology product aimed at consumers came to me to ask advice on how to launch his product. He had a budget of about $400,000 for the year. Not enough to put him into the big leagues, but certainly enough to make an impact with his target audience.

His plan, and I'm not making this up, was to buy a one-minute commercial on *The Cosby Show* (this was a while ago). At the time, this was the most popular show on television, and it offered one of the simplest, most efficient ways to reach the largest number of consumers.

He planned to spend his entire budget on one commercial

and then cease advertising for a year while he coasted on the enormous sales the ad would generate.

From his point of view, the reasoning was solid. He had a great product with a neat story to tell. He believed he could relate the story in one minute and that anyone hearing the story would instantly want what he sold. Because he was in a hurry to beat his competition to market, his thinking was that he should reach the maximum number of people in the short-est possible time and then rely on the overwhelming power of his product to generate sales.

Of course, this is a ridiculous strategy, and he realized it before he spent his entire budget on nonsense. It was entirely ludicrous because very few people tuning in to *Cosby* were his ideal customers. Those who were most likely to buy might not watch the commercial closely. And if they did, it's unlikely that with just one exposure to his marvelous message they'd rush out and buy his product.

Here's another way to think about the problem of reach versus frequency. Imagine you have a packet with one hundred flower seeds in it. Also pretend you've been given one hundred watering cans each filled with just enough water to soak one seed for a few days.

It seems as though you could do one of two things. You could plant all one hundred seeds and then water each seed one time. My guess is that every single seed would then fail to grow. Or you could plant just twenty seeds and then throw the other eighty in the trash. Water each of the twenty seeds five times over the course of a week and you'd probably end up with twenty flowers.

Marketers hate to throw away perfectly good seeds. They

want their advertising to be seen far and wide. Unfortunately, until recently they had to pick between reach and frequency.

The problem with frequency is that it's expensive. Two ads on *Seinfeld* cost about twice as much as one ad. Two ads in *Time* magazine cost about twice as much as one ad. Two direct mail letters cost exactly twice as much as one. You can't have both reach and frequency in the old media. With a fixed budget, marketers had to choose.

So there's a huge trade-off in most media. When you use Interruption Marketing to drive home a message, you've got to decide whether you should target a new prospect, someone you hope will sit up and take notice of your clever and novel advertising, someone who will jump up and say, "My God, I've been waiting for this product all my life, where do I sign up!" or, for virtually the same cost, whether you should market to someone who ignored you the last time you tried to sell them something. Faced with the choice of the cheap and easy ah-ha! sale or the frequent, persistent, dripping water sale, many marketers choose the former.

Back to Muhammad Ali again. After he's hit someone ten times and the guy's still standing, the opportunity for the quick knockout is long gone. Only through persistence is Ali going to get this guy down. The easy path is no longer available. Yet the path that remains is the one that works: frequency.

So even though frequency is expensive, it still must be used. The reason national advertisers need to spend so much money (Procter & Gamble spent more than $2 *billion* last year) is that without reach and frequency, you can't build a national brand.

Marketing guru Jay Levinson figures you have to run an ad twenty-seven times against one individual before it has its desired impact. Why? Because only one out of nine ads is seen, and you've got to see it at least three times before it sinks in.

The last thing that gets in the way of most marketers is that they spend too much time running popularity contests regarding the creative content of the ads they run. They show them around the office, quiz the janitor, and frame the ads and put them on the walls. Instead of focusing on ads that work, they focus on ads that are cool.

Pick up an issue of *USA Today* and you're likely to see reviews of commercials. Reviews! Go to the water cooler at work after the Super Bowl and you're likely to hear people complaining about a boring ad run by one company and how cool and engaging another ad was for something else.

An ad agency that tells its client to leave its ads untouched for months, or even weeks, is seen as incompetent or lazy. Let's face it—it's fun to make new commercials, fun to reach loads of people, and fun to create ads that are the talk of the ad community or the country.

The only person who should decide when you change your advertising is your accountant! When the ad stops working, when the look ceases to be profitable, change it.

Direct marketers know this because they measure everything they do. The L. L. Bean catalog is a monument to frequency. Loyal customers have each received more than three hundred catalogs over the last thirty years, and every single one of them was a lot like the last one they'd received.

Whenever you feel as though frequency isn't the answer,

Frequency–Related Marketing Problems

1. Because people don't pay attention to advertising, ads that run without a lot of frequency are ignored.
2. Because marketers must interrupt a busy consumer, advertising carries a lot of fluff and sizzle along with the message, so there isn't a lot of room to tell a compelling story.
3. Because consumers are overwhelmed with data, they ignore or misunderstand most new concepts.
4. Frequency is extremely expensive, and it's tempting to focus on untouched consumers instead of those who haven't yet responded.
5. Running ads frequently is boring.

---

imagine that you're a calculus teacher with two choices: 1) interrupt a school pep rally to give a one-minute lecture on integrals to all 1,000 students in the school; or 2) get thirty minutes of uninterrupted attention from the fifty best students in the school, all of whom are just the right level for your class and all of whom need to get an A in your class in order to get into college.

While the first group will undoubtedly give you greater reach, it's fairly certain that no one will learn any calculus. The second group, on the other hand, presented with relevant information that captures their devoted attention, is far more likely to get the message.

Another problem reach marketers have when it comes to frequency is that most media are optimized to reach a small percentage of the viewing audience. Some people *never* open their junk mail. Some people *never* watch TV commercials.

Some people online (actually about half) have never ever clicked on a Web banner. So the thought of advertising to these people again and again is quite scary.

Some marketers wonder, "If the best prospects have already understood my ads and then ignored them, doesn't repeating those same ads with frequency only leave me with the bottom of the barrel—the least likely, the least receptive, the hardest to reach?" It turns out that the answer to that question is "no." You don't reach the bottom of the barrel. You do reach the most profitable prospects with frequency.

Imagine the poor popcorn salesman at the hockey game. He walks up and down the aisles, schlepping his popcorn basket up and down the stairs. Given the choice, the popcorn guy will cover as many sections as he possibly can rather than working one section repeatedly. He believes that the best prospects raise their hands early. Because he has a monopoly, he can afford to skim the cream, to get the easy sales and then go home. His profitability isn't based on converting non–popcorn eaters into popcorn eaters.

Given the very high cost of frequency to the popcorn guy (every minute he stays in one section is a minute not spent with a new group), along with the clear dichotomy between buyers and nonbuyers, it's probably a good strategy.

But what if he had a team of fifty salespeople working for him? What if he could give out free samples? What if it were easier and cheaper for him to talk with nonpopcorn folks with frequency? What would happen if once he converted someone to the joys of popcorn, he could sell a box of popcorn to that new convert every game for the rest of the season?

Unfortunately it's rare to be in the position of the pop-corn guy. It's far more likely that you're selling a more compli-cated product, in a far more cluttered market. If so, you'll win by figuring out how to make your frequency more effective. Permission Marketing will allow you to do this.

Permission Empowers Frequency

Permission Marketing is the tool that makes frequency work. But before going into why that's true, it's important to preface the discussion with a little bit more about the nature of brand trust. Here are some examples of trusted national brands that have dutifully performed the requisite steps to earn trust: Crisco, Tabasco, Campbell's, Vaseline, and Arm & Hammer.

If you're like most Americans, you have every single one of these products in your house. And every one of them was launched more than fifty years ago. Fifty years! This isn't the newest or the coolest or the hippest or the cheapest. These are products you chose because you trust them.

Why do you trust them? Because of frequency. Because over the years you've seen their ads, encountered them in restaurants (and even art galleries), eaten them at friends' houses, and generally been inundated with frequent messages about their quality and reliability.

All of these brands are now coasting. They do relatively little advertising, and the advertising they do isn't very inno-vative or aggressive. But because they've used fifty-plus years of frequency in a focused, consistent way, they've made a huge impact on you and virtually every other consumer in this country.

Because they're trusted, they're profitable. In fact, in virtually every industry *the most trusted brand is also the most profitable*. Frequency led to awareness, awareness to familiarity, and familiarity to trust. And trust, almost without exception, leads to profit.

But what if you're not Vaseline? What if your product isn't a piece of our culture, and you need to build that trust?

The need for frequency in advertising means that you can't market a product in one fell swoop. Instead it's an interactive process, an approach that takes time and persistence and continual adjustment. This portends a new way of thinking about marketing. And it may go against the way we were raised to think about work and about our expectations of how things are done.

A neat way to understand this is to remember your school. Over the generations, elementary school has served as a window on the way our culture works. Two hundred years ago people worked as craftsmen. They had few mechanical devices, worked on just a few products at a time, and turned out objects that were unique and of very high quality.

School was sort of like that as well. The one-room schoolhouse was the domain of a single talented individual. Her job was to work with each student individually and, after a few years, turn out students who had actually learned something.

Then the Industrial Revolution occurred and we changed our work habits to include factories, and that change infiltrated our concept of schools. Instead of relying on a unique individual to shape a few students, we built school factories.

Each room is like a workstation in a factory assembly line. The desks are lined up in rows. Teachers teach from a standardized curriculum. Instead of being rewarded as crafts-men, they're hired for their ability to follow instructions. And at the end of each semester, the students move to the next stop on the assembly line.

Students who don't fit their "batch" on the assembly line are removed to special programs. Students who don't meet the quality standards set by a centralized quality-control facility are disciplined, repaired, or rejected. The teachers' union, just like the autoworkers' union, pushes for ever more standard-ization and job protection.

Schools haven't changed very much, but marketing has. Marketing can no longer work as a series of events in which the next ad is stamped out and the result is a measurable uptick in sales. Instead, successful marketers have turned ad-vertising into an interactive process. Using relationships and frequency and permission, it's now profitable to fundamen-tally change the assembly-line/event-perspective into a long-term process, a continually adjusted program that zigs and zags and grows and adapts.

It's no longer "Run an ad on Tuesday, watch sales go up on Wednesday." Advertisers don't have the power to interrupt enough consumers to make it pay the way it used to.

In a world of mass customization, of high-speed products and higher-speed messaging, consumers don't want an off-the-shelf batch approach. Just as consumers are now demand-ing more personalization (from one hundred coffee drinks at Starbucks to thousands of different models from Nike), they are most likely to respond to advertising that is frequent, fo-cused, and personal.

Was it more efficient to build things in batches? Definitely.

Just as it was probably more efficient to educate kids in batches. But the days of high demand and limited supply are over. We are no longer competing to see who can build the factories that will supply the world.

It's a new game now. A game in which the limited supply is attention, not factories.

Creating value through interaction is far more important than solving a consumer's problem in thirty seconds. So if you can get the right to communicate with permission, you've just obtained the right to use frequency. And that, as we've seen, is the holy grail of marketing.

Many marketers are uncomfortable with this change. But others are embracing it and finding vast profits as a result.

Permission Marketing is not a ready, aim, fire approach to marketing. At its core, it flies in the face of traditional thinking about advertising. The great marketers of the fifties and sixties knew how to interrupt people. They knew how to craft a campaign that would gain attention and, in just a few moments, communicate a basic idea. They spent a lot of time building interruption into their marketing and then made their ideas simple enough that they could be communicated in the short time left over.

Just as important, they had the guts to use frequency to make their ads work. Those memorable VW Beetle ads were consistent and frequent. The ads for Starkist Tuna and Frosted Flakes were omnipresent. Mass marketers had a solution to our problems and were disciplined enough to drive it home again and again. We all remember these classic ad campaigns because they were delivered to us with massive frequency in an environment that had a fraction of the clutter we face today.

Permission Marketing allows the same effectiveness. It encourages the commitment and frequency that made mass marketing work years ago. But it replaces continuing interruption with ongoing interaction.

What if frequency were free? What if you could cut through the clutter and know that the recipient of your next advertising message was actually going to pay attention? What if you knew that instead of focusing your advertising on the sizzle, you could make it all steak?

Remember that calculus teacher? If she's got the right students, and they're properly motivated by a genuine quest to learn (or to get an A), she has permission to teach to them with frequency. She doesn't have to spend a lot of time telling jokes, showing filmstrips, or going on field trips. She has their attention.

Now, because she knows who they are and what they want, she can engage them in dialogue. She can learn what they know and what they don't know. She can deliver the missing pieces. She can use frequency to drive home a message.

The power that comes from frequency is obviously enormous. The only barrier was how inefficient it was. But with Permission Marketing, for the first time in this arena of growing clutter, frequency is effective and efficient.

Every direct marketer and catalog marketer has an A list. This is the list of people who buy proportionally more products than the rest of the population. When the J. Peterman or the Lands' End catalog arrives on the A-list customer's doorstep, attention is paid. Orders are given. The prospect trusts the merchant, the prospect buys from the merchant. Without realizing it, these direct marketers have built a permission-based relationship with these customers. Is it any surprise they buy more?

Is the permission overt? Did the consumer say, "Please, go ahead and send catalogs"? Well, not quite. But by buying from these catalogs, by rewarding the frequent interruptions with business again and again, these consumers now anticipate the catalog. They've decided that the catalog is relevant to them, and they hold off on purchases until the next catalog comes.

Imagine how much better the A list would be if there were explicit rewards and overt permission instead of the more subtle relationship that exists today.

Permission Marketing is a disciplined process that allows any marketer to find the same level of attention and effectiveness with its prospects. By overtly creating benefits in exchange for giving permission, and then delivering on the promises made, virtually every marketer can dramatically increase the effectiveness of its frequency—and deliver it at a lower cost.

In essence, Permission Marketing takes the efficiency that comes from having prospects pay attention and turns the savings into frequency. Once you know that the vast majority of people you target *want* to hear from you, frequency starts looking pretty attractive. And when you can use the power of the new media to deliver that frequency for free, you hit a home run.

The biggest secret of the Internet is that it is inherently a direct marketing medium. In fact, the Internet is the greatest direct marketing medium of all time. In a later chapter you'll see exactly how poorly the Web succeeds at interrupting people.

E-mail is the main reason people use the Internet. And e-mail delivers frequency for free. Permission Marketing will allow you to harvest that frequency.

Time and again, marketing surveys demonstrate that people are likely to patronize businesses they trust. Consumers have very strong feelings about many of the brands and services in their lives, and generally, trust is the critical prerequisite.

Where does trust come from? Trust comes from frequency. But before frequency turns into sales, it turns into permission. Permission to communicate, permission to customize, permission to teach. And permission is just a step away from trust.

SIX

The Five Levels of Permission

You want fries with that, sir?

T EN YEARS AGO your neighborhood milkman was about as passé a marketing concept as they get. He was a punch line in a joke about wayward women. Today, though, the milkman is back. Streamline delivers groceries. Columbia Record Club sends CDs. And yes, the milkman delivers milk. All without asking each time.

All permission is not created equal. Remember when you were "dating" in second grade? It meant you had permission to hold hands, but only sometimes, and only if there weren't too many people around. That's a little different level of permission compared with that of a couple going steady in college.

The goal of the Permission Marketer is to move consumers up the permission ladder, moving them from strangers to friends to customers. And from customers to loyal customers. At every step up the ladder, trust grows, responsibility grows, and profits grow.

There are five levels of permission. The highest level of permission is called the "intravenous" level. The fifth and lowest is called the "situation" level. Here are the five levels in order of importance.

1. Intravenous (and "purchase-on-approval" model)
2. Points (liability model and chance model)
3. Personal relationships
4. Brand trust
5. Situation

There's a sixth level, but it's so low I won't even refer to it as a level at all. It's called spam (unsolicited advertising), and it's covered last.

THE INTRAVENOUS PERMISSION LEVEL

The highest level of permission is called "intravenous." This is what you've got going when you're in the intensive care unit with a needle in your arm and a bag of medicine dripping into your veins.

Your doctor has your written permission to inject just about anything he wants into your IV bag. Not only can he select and administer the drug, but he can then charge you for the treatment and fully expect that you'll pay for it.

A marketer who has achieved intravenous permission from his customer is making the buying decisions on behalf of the consumer. The privilege is huge, but the downside is significant. If the marketer guesses wrong or, worse, abuses the permission, it will be canceled in a heartbeat.

The insanely profitable law firms of the 1980s made their money using this level of Permission Marketing. Wealthy corporations gave them what were essentially blank checks, along with permission to engage in whatever activities were in the interest of the company. Further, they didn't ask what anything cost and didn't question the legal bills.

Some of those firms nurtured and cared for this permission and turned themselves into multimillion-dollar enterprises. Others abused it, lived high for a while, but were inexplicably surprised when the companies got smart and started questioning what was happening.

Fifty years ago perhaps the single most profitable player in the book publishing world was the Book of the Month Club. Why were they so profitable? Because they had permission to choose a book and send it, with an invoice, to millions and millions of people. The club was similar to the book clubs you see today, except there were fewer choices and the vast majority of recipients accepted the selected book. The book selection committee was composed of well-known literati, and it was considered an honor to be on their board. The public basically gave them wide-ranging permission to choose and then ship whatever book they chose.

Clever marketing and excellent taste had earned them the right to choose, print, ship, and bill books to a public that was eager to read their selections. With this base of intravenous permission, the club's board had enormous power. A main selection could make an author's career. The club wasn't afraid to use this power, either. They relentlessly drove their costs down, acquiring books for a fraction of what they'd cost in a bookstore. But selling them, of course, at nearly full price.

By acting on the consumer's behalf, they took great care with the permission they were granted and built ever more permission from their base. It was only the splintering of American interests, together with the evil reign of TV, that led to the eventual decline in their power.

The folks at Poland Springs have that same level of permission with the water cooler in our office. Automatic replenishment systems allow oil heating vendors and others to invest money up front to acquire permission and then extract profits for years down the road by not violating the trust they've earned.

Magazine subscriptions are another great example of this model. Each issue you receive is paid for *before* you read it. Consumers give magazine publishers permission to send them a booklet full of ads and articles each month, and they agree to pay for it in advance.

Why would anyone do this? Why give up so much control and allow someone else to profit from this level of trust?

The first reason, which is becoming ever more important, is to save time. Streamline would fail if America went back to having one spouse stay at home all day. Instead of paying Streamline to collect your groceries, dry cleaning, and photographs, you'd invest a few hours and save a few dollars by doing it yourself. But because Streamline can save the consumer such a precious resource, we gladly pay them a premium in exchange for the time we save.

The second reason is to save money. In many industries the cost of marketing is the single largest line item in the cost of goods. A magazine might cost three times as much on the newsstand as it does by subscription. Automatic deposit of your paycheck costs a fraction of what a check-cashing bodega charges.

This cost-saving approach appears in a wide range of areas. For example, in exchange for eliminating their risk and saving the sales cost, Procter & Gamble gives Wal-Mart a huge discount on Tide detergent. P&G gets complete access to Wal-Mart's cash register database and actually delivers new Tide to Wal-Mart stores without even receiving a purchase order.

By giving P&G permission to put Tide in any Wal-Mart whenever they like, Wal-Mart saves time and money.

The third reason is a little more surprising. Many consumers sign up for intravenous permission because they don't like to make a choice. The Book of the Month Club virtually guaranteed that you'd be able to read what everyone else was reading. The patient in the hospital doesn't want to compare drugs.

As computers make it easier for marketers to understand and catalog the various individual nuances among customers, this reason will become increasingly important. The more successful the marketer is at selecting products that are relevant to our lives, the more likely we're willing to let them pick.

The fourth reason is to avoid stock outs. The milkman makes sure we never run out of milk. Same with the guy who delivers water for the water cooler. The opportunities in this arena are huge. Imagine a laser printer (hooked up to your network, of course) that automatically reorders toner cartridges by e-mail when it's running low. Or a car that beeps the factory by cellular circuit when it's time for them to send someone to tune it up in your driveway, while you and your family are sleeping.

The idea of automatic replenishment can be extended in more ways as technology makes it easier to execute these systems. Virtually every product, therefore, can be sold by subscription!

I wasn't surprised to discover that Gateway just announced computers by subscription, a concept I've been touting for a few years. Instead of buying a computer and taking your chances, you just pay them $49 a month and every two years they upgrade you to the latest and greatest model. Expect to see this happen in more and more industries.

After all, you may not really want a particular car as much as you just want reliable transportation. So instead of leasing a car for a given period of time, you could just pay Ford a monthly fee and give them permission to put the right car, filled with gas and running well, in your driveway every day. As long as Ford is keeping up their half of the bargain, you'll be willing to listen to whatever new offer they choose to bring your way.

Purchase on Approval

Of course, not all intravenous marketing is quite this automatic. There's a second level called "purchase-on-approval." In this model, a second level of authorization is required before the consumer is actually billed. This is far more common than full intravenous, and you're doubtless signed up for some of this already.

When Columbia Record Club chooses a record album for you, for example, they send you a note about what the automatic selection will be next month. If you choose to say "no," they don't ship. If they've guessed your needs correctly, it comes automatically.

Marketers often call this a "negative option." It's often used with great success by continuity programs, though it's occasionally misused. Credit cards, for example, have made it very easy for marketers to get a significant amount of permission with automatic billing. The problem arises when a marketer hopes (and even expects) that the consumer will forget he gave this negative option permission and they generate years and years of revenue with nothing delivered in exchange.

Prodigy's most profitable customers during their heyday, for example, were individuals who joined with a credit card and never used the service! Month after month consumers were billed for something they didn't use, and because it was added automatically to a charge card bill, many never noticed (in fact, there are tens of thousands of people who have been paying this bill for more than a decade).

Cendant (formerly CUC) makes a huge amount of money with the same technique. Individuals join the Shopper's Advantage or other buying clubs, paying a $49 annual fee to belong. With excellent marketing they've been able to attract tens of millions of members. But instead of working hard to upgrade the permission at every step, these marketers often rely on the invisibility of the credit card payment to generate an annuity.

Prodigy and Cendant and others are squandering a huge permission opportunity. They've already done the hard part. They've gained access to the consumer and her credit card. They have the right to upsell these consumers in a focused, relevant, expected way. The challenge is to use that permission to upgrade the amount of attention and profit that can be extracted.

But purchase-on-approval is more than just negative option. A salesperson at Nordstrom, for example, often earns permission to call or write when a special item comes in. Or a great bookstore clerk might remember a customer's preferences and call when the new Elmore Leonard arrives.

Amazon.com intends to build the next level of their business around purchase-on-approval. By understanding the needs and desires of their customers, and by earning the permission to talk to this audience, they can use collaborative filtering—using a computer to figure out the likelihood that you'll like something new based on your past purchases—to alert you to a book you might want to try. They can even use (gasp) a human being to make recommendations!

In many ways, purchase-on-approval is the most powerful form of permission that many marketers will ever achieve. While it lacks the sexiness of full intravenous, it does provide a wide-open channel between the busy consumer and the marketer who needs to reach him.

Even with this high level of permission, consumers are always subject to poaching. The marketer can't become complacent or, worse, begin taking advantage of the permission.

I used to be a regular customer of a framing store in town. I never even looked at the price he charged me, because over time he had learned what I liked and I had determined that he always treated me fairly.

On a recent trip, though, I discovered that another customer, one less loyal than I, was getting a better price. Fear of that customer's shopping around had led the framer to give him a discount.

Seeing this, I felt betrayed. I said nothing to the framer, but realizing how I was being punished for my loyalty, I've now become a price-conscious framing customer again.

Customers want more than price. They want a combination of price and service and safety and comfort. If that mix is superior to your competitor's, you will be able to maintain this enviable level of permission. But be wary of taking the permission for granted. If it is valuable to you, it's also valuable to your competitors.

Sometimes, even after you've achieved intravenous permission, you'll need to offer consumers added inducements to pay attention.

THE POINTS PERMISSION LEVEL

The next level of permission is points. Points are a formalized, scalable approach to attracting and keeping the prospect's attention.

Remember S&H Green Stamps? What a great idea. Every time you purchased a product at a participating store, you got some stamps. You licked them and put them into little booklets. Fill up enough booklets and you were eligible for a free gift.

The department store used the stamps as a way of rewarding loyalty and building frequency. After all, just a few stamps were worthless. But if you came back again and again, they suddenly gained in value.

Of course, the more alert retailer would use Green Stamps

to modify consumer behavior and, specifically, to reward consumers for paying attention. For example, it's not hard to imagine offering bonus Green Stamps to anyone who buys Donna Karan shoes today. Even if I wasn't about to buy a pair of shoes, I'm certainly likely to check them out if I'm collecting the points you're offering. The offer of a reward in exchange for my patronage (and by extension my attention) is powerful indeed.

Think about how much more efficient this is than putting something on sale. Instead of having to give a huge discount (basically a cash payment) and gaining no long-term benefit, the merchant can give away just a few of the points and not only get attention today, but build a program that's even more likely to work tomorrow.

The best marketing programs get better over time. They don't depend on novelty to burst through the clutter, nor do they build on a foundation that doesn't actually deliver value in the long run. Green Stamps worked for decades because they were based on a solid principle and the concept was well executed.

The more you collected Green Stamps, the more you collected Green Stamps. This is an essential tautology for any points program. They must be constructed in a way that earning ever more points is easier and more compelling. Points marketers love to give away rewards, because it means that the program is working.

Green Stamps became a currency. And like all currencies, they acquired a particular value. Marketers got to decide exactly how much currency they were willing to spend for attention and ultimately for a sale.

This is a critical component of a points system and one of the reasons this level of permission is so exciting. It's almost impossible to quantify the cost (and value) of a TV campaign. Putting products on sale or paying your salespeople a spiff may indeed move more product, but it's essentially impossible to determine exactly how much currency you need to spend to get what you want.

Points solve that problem. Points have a cost (in the case of Green Stamps, the cost is the amount you have to pay the centralized organization for every stamp you buy and then give to a consumer). And points have a result. Spend more points, get more results. And that changes this from a spin of the wheel to a predictable, testable science.

By applying a points currency that is exactly congruent with the needs of the people you're trying to reach in the first place, you can make the offer significantly more efficient. Offering millionaires a free garbage disposal, for example, is incongruent. It won't attract enough of the people you want, nor will it change the behavior of the few who do notice it.

Because different people have different attention thresholds, cash discounts are a crude form of points. Frequently the discount is given to someone who could have lived happily without it. Other times the discount is insufficient to get an ideal prospect to buy from you the first time.

Because points work at so many levels, and because they get more and more valuable as an attention meter over time, they overcome the problems of a cash discount or a noisy TV ad.

Inherent in any points program is a flexible method to reward consumers for paying attention or for buying something. It's pretty straightforward to track and reward buying behavior. Even the ice-cream store in my hometown offers a card that offers a free cone after you buy ten. By punching your card with every visit, they can accurately track patronage and build loyalty and frequency.

Rewarding consumers for paying attention, however, is hard. Proving that an individual paid attention is difficult, especially if there's a large audience. What's worse is the opportunity for fraud. If you can earn points by leaving your TV on or clicking a mouse button, it's pretty easy to bust open a system with substantial rewards.

When I first developed the ideas behind Permission Marketing, I took my own advice and started a company focused on using these techniques online. Yoyodyne's entire approach to Permission Marketing is structured around points programs that reward consumers for their attention. By offering additional entries (points) toward a great prize, Yoyodyne is able to capture and manipulate the attention of consumers.

Best of all, the cost of each point is close to zero. By creating a currency that has a high value to consumers but a very low cost to marketers, we've figured out a way to generate an attention economy that works for everyone.

The results are nothing short of extraordinary. After getting permission from a consumer, Yoyodyne responds with a series of e-mail messages, focused on teaching the prospect about a sponsor's message.

The company averages a 36 percent response rate to these mailings, with a few promotions earning more than 60 percent. For perspective, compare this with the typical direct mail campaign (in which you have to buy the envelopes, printing, and stamps!): About 2 percent is considered terrific.

How can something as simple as points lead to an 1,800 percent increase in responsiveness? How can prosaic prizes and straightforward sweepstakes do such a great job of modifying consumer behavior?

The answer most critics supply is that points programs don't really work. They say that paying people for their attention, or to take action, might work sometimes, but more often these programs encourage people to fake it, to read an ad but not for the right reasons.

While this seems logical, it is completely wrong. In several audited studies and side-by-side tests, we've been able to show that consumers are just as likely (and in some cases more likely) to actually purchase, and then repurchase, than consumers who are interrupted by conventional means.

AVOIDING THE "OPPORTUNITY SEEKERS": EVERYONE WANTS SOMETHING

Perhaps the biggest criticism I've heard of Permission Marketing techniques is that people believe they will attract the dreaded "Opportunity Seekers." Of course, all of us are seeking opportunities, but in the mailing list business an Opportunity Seeker (capital O, capital S) is someone with more time than money, a nonconsumer who focuses on low-margin items and is a less than ideal prospect for most products.

Any mailing list broker will tell you the profile of an Opportunity Seeker (and be happy to rent you their names). This group tends to be lower income, and they tend to skew older than the ideal marketing demographic. Not the type of demographic a high-margin marketer salivates over.

Lillian Vernon sells to Opportunity Seekers. J. Peterman does not.

Opportunity Seekers enter sweepstakes like crazy. They often read newsletters about how to win, and they're the first people on the block to fall for a Ponzi scheme or a cleverly written but misleading or untruthful mailing for house siding or weight-loss fads. When you see some poor schmo on TV who was duped into losing his life savings, you've found an Opportunity Seeker.

A marketing technique designed to attract the attention and loyalty of this group isn't worth much. But in reality, the reason a marketer will get opt-in participation from any group is always based on the selfish, greed-focused nature of the benefits offered. Savvy marketers argue that this is an inherent flaw in building a marketing campaign around this technique because it will bring in the wrong people, the folks who will waste your time but not pay the money.

Does offering something of immediate value in exchange for attention always lead to responses from the lowest common denominator? My answer to this comes in the form of a question: Do you collect frequent flier miles?

If you're like most upwardly mobile or even wealthy individuals, you do. You can afford that vacation in Paris, yet you willingly give up your privacy to allow American (or one of its competitors) to track where you fly.

In addition, you might even carry an American Airlines credit card (Citibank AAdvantage card is one of the most popular in the country). This card trades whatever privacy you had left in exchange for a few more miles.

With hundreds of millions of dollars spent marketing

sweepstakes, contests, and affinity programs last year, there's no question that they work. But it's also true that Opportunity Seekers are not the core group of people participating!

At a recent conference of executives, I took a poll. There were two questions:

1. How many of you have enough money in the bank to pay for your own vacation this year?
2. How many of you aggressively track your frequent flier miles?

The answer to the first question was almost 100 percent "yes." To the second, I got a "yes" as well, but I discovered that the audience also altered hotel schedules, credit card plans, and even flight arrangements to maximize their mileage.

Part of the attraction of the miles programs is that they offer users a sense of mastery. It's easy to feel smart about the way you're using miles. You can understand and even try to beat the system.

Along the way, American and other airlines have basically invented a new currency, and it is a currency they can trade for attention. To date, however, the airlines have been remarkably crude at leveraging that permission.

For example, American knows that I fly only to San Francisco. I've been telling them that every time I fly, and they have banks of computers that know everywhere I go (and not just me—you too). Yet the mailings that come in my frequent flier packet every month are identical to my neighbor's, who travels only by bus (he uses his credit card to get the miles and trades them in for hotel stays).

What a waste of my attention! If they sent me coupons for restaurants in San Francisco or the opportunity to buy a guidebook or to stay in a special hotel—that would have an effect on me. Instead they've built up a huge permission base and are squandering an important component of it.

Yes, it is difficult and expensive to get someone to sign up for and then become fascinated by a points program. Yes, it's unlikely you'll get as many sign-ups as the airlines did. But for those industries in which a points program can be implemented, it's a remarkably inexpensive way to attract and keep exactly the right people.

Sometimes even smart marketers fall into the trap of projecting their own current wants and desires onto the population at large. Maybe *you* wouldn't cross the street to win a thousand dollars or even a T-shirt. But we've seen again and again that consumers want the recognition and frisson of winning that comes from participating in these programs.

Like S&H Green Stamps, frequent flier miles are a huge success because consumers can incrementally win discounts and awards. And the incremental nature of the program allows large numbers of people to participate in a quick and easy way.

Gtech, the leading creator of lotteries and lottery tickets, has discovered a terrific insight. When a lottery prize exceeds a certain level (about $5 million), an entirely new audience of players participates. Have you ever bought a lottery ticket? Most readers of this book have. But I'll bet only for the big prizes.

If the reward is big enough, if the participation is easy

enough, if the odds seem good enough, if there's enough trust—just about everybody wants to win something. Just about everyone wants to save a buck.

My favorite example of this is the airline that was trying to build a hub in Saudi Arabia. Their goal was to get extremely wealthy (and very busy) travelers to alter their travel plans and make a connection through Saudi Arabia. Their solution was simple. They gave away a Rolls-Royce every day to one lucky first-class passenger.

It seems to me that few rich people would invest their most valuable asset—time—in order to win a prize they could probably afford if they really wanted it. Yet the promotion worked. And it worked in a big way.

So why do they work? In my company's experience, it's because consumers have a good time. They feel smart. They feel in control. They feel safe. They like getting me-mail, not e-mail (every interaction is anticipated, personal, and relevant, not to mention unique, to them).

Yoyodyne participants are twice as likely to have a college degree as the population at large. These are smart people who like to be reminded that they're smart. They also like to try to beat the system. A points-based promotion can do all of those things.

Points programs can be divided into two categories: liability and chance.

THE POINT LIABILITY MODEL

In liability programs, every point delivered has a real value. A Green Stamp or a frequent flier mile is actually worth something—get enough and you can trade it in for something, guaranteed.

The good news is that consumers like this. It eliminates fears of fraud or scams and makes it easy for a consumer to feel as though he or she is making progress toward the reward that had been signed up for in the first place.

The downside comes with the cost to the marketer. If every point earned costs money, then the cost of modifying behavior can be significant. At last count, for example, the airlines were carrying billions of dollars in liability as a result of their programs. If all the miles were permitted to be redeemed, there would be no room for paying passengers and the airlines would be literally bankrupt.

The way a marketer deals with this issue has a huge impact on the validity of the program. The airlines, for example, have gotten away with dramatically limiting the number of seats available for frequent flier redemptions. This certainly isn't in the spirit of the program's original intent, and now, for all intents and purposes, the airlines are giving away miles that they have no intention of ever redeeming. It's beginning to feel like a pyramid scheme, in which the new users are funding the travel of the original ones.

As long as consumers don't lose faith in the program, it will continue to prosper. The airlines are responding to some consumer anxiety by making more seats available on more flights at the last minute, thus maintaining their paying base but still giving consumers confidence that there really is a pot of gold at the end of the rainbow.

Some liability programs don't offer a reward at all. Instead consumers work to earn greater discounts on future purchases, but these discounts still lead to self-liquidating re-wards. Buy three boxes of Cheerios and get this great Frisbee for just $3 in postage and handling! Fortunately the $3 often covers the entire cost of the postage, the handling, and the Frisbee.

Self-liquidating premiums or discounts provide some flash, and like the decoder rings our parents collected in the 1950s, they work sometimes. The real risk comes when the consumer doesn't value the item very much. When that happens, the points become worthless.

Implicit in the liability model is that because the marginal value of another point is significant, fraud prevention is critical. There are great examples of glitches in the system in which you could earn more in miles than what it cost in the actual ticket price. Smart consumers responded by racking up miles and subverting the intent of the system.

One way that marketers work to avoid fraud is by focusing on actual purchases and rarely if ever rewarding consumers for attention.

If you reward a consumer for attention, and the reward is tangible enough, the consumer can fake the attention, or hire a stand-in, or program a computer to beat the system. This is extremely unlikely in the point chance model, but it's easy to see how the liability approach can lead to this.

THE POINT CHANCE MODEL

The chance model is almost a reverse of the liability model. Consumers don't earn a guaranteed reward; instead they earn more chances to *win* a reward. Sort of like getting lots and lots of lottery tickets, for free, in exchange for a desired behavior.

The biggest advantage of the chance model is that the cost of one more point is basically zero. If the prize is fixed (win $1 million or win a free car), then inflating the number of entries doesn't cost the marketer anything at all.

The biggest disadvantage is directly related to the advantage: If a consumer doesn't think he has a chance to win, he's not going to enter. And one step further, if it isn't fun to keep playing, he'll walk.

So the challenge of the chance marketer is to create a series of events, promotions, and interactions that battle the compression that sets in. By constantly raising the stakes and making winning more likely and the prizes more compelling, chance marketers can maintain the interest and continue modifying the behavior of target consumers.

Once a lottery passes a $5 million prize, it attracts a completely different audience. Suddenly a totally new demographic is focused on winning the prize—doctors, lawyers, and other upper-middle-income households begin to realize that a prize of that magnitude really could change their lives.

Points programs with a chance element must do the same thing. The prize must be so life changing and so relevant to a particular consumer that it cuts through the clutter, gets people to sign up, and, of greatest importance, leads to frequency.

When it works, it is powerful indeed. In Yoyodyne's Web-surfing promotion, Get Rich Click, the average consumer visits more than five Web sites that we select for them. In EZSpree, our shopping promotion, the average consumer visited six stores, clicked through on more than 20 percent of them, and a full 14 percent of the participants actually went ahead and made an online purchase through the promotion.

These numbers are orders of magnitude higher than other consumer behaviors on the Web, and the reasons are simple:

1. No one enters a promotion thinking he's going to lose.
2. No one quits a promotion when she's tied for first place.
3. The fear of losing because you don't have enough points outweighs the cost of attention that comes from performing in the way the marketer asks.
4. If the interactions are fun and good for the ego, it's likely the consumer will continue to participate.

As you consider points programs for your business, keep several factors in mind. The first challenge is to build in a steep reward curve to ensure loyalty. American Airlines gives almost nothing to people who fly once every few months. But once you push the envelope just a little bit further, the upgrades to business class and other perks start to kick in.

Second—and this is critical—the program must be built with permission overtly included. Consumers must understand from the first day that the marketer will be watching their actions and will be using the data to send focused, relevant, personal messages to them.

Without permission, a reward to the consumer is worth far less to the marketer. So it's important to define the permission very carefully. Is it transferable? American Airlines knows a lot about you—what can they do with that data? The goal is to avoid surprising the consumers and interacting with them by sending only messages they expect.

Technology is permitting a number of hybrids. These are less overt than points programs but capture many of the same benefits.

Catalina, for example, has placed a computer into more than 80 percent of all the supermarkets in America. The computer monitors the UPC codes of every purchase made by every consumer in that store. It also notes the bar code on your check-cashing or store discount card.

What can it do with that data? Using a special printer at every checkout, it can print a string of coupons designed just for you. If you buy Häagen-Dazs, for example, it can print out a Ben & Jerry's coupon. Who better to deliver that coupon to, after all, than someone who just proved he loves this category?

Of course, Catalina can go much, much further. Once you've used your bonus card, they know who you are. Where you live. How much you spend in the store every week and what you usually buy.

Now, the permission that you granted when you filled out and then started using the bonus card doesn't clearly grant them the right to go ahead and track all of this. On the other hand, they bend over backward not to surprise the consumer with clever parlor tricks (like sending a congratulatory letter to your house after noticing that you and your husband were buying baby food and size one diapers for a few weeks).

In working to make the offers relevant and personalized, Catalina can vary the number of "points" they give you. For example, it's easy for them to give very loyal Kellogg's customers a bigger coupon for Quaker Oats than they give to someone who is more likely to shop around.

They can alter the points based on where you live, how much you buy, or even, in a completely closed loop, how often you've redeemed their coupons in the past! Ignore a few coupons in a row and they might test to see what happens when they offer to give you a competitor's product for *free*.

The important distinction here is that while Catalina has access to *data,* they really don't have that much *permission.* Without the permission, it's hard for them to fully realize the value here. Imagine how much more profitable they could be if the consumers were eagerly anticipating the messages they were sending.

THE PERSONAL RELATIONSHIP LEVEL

The third level of permission is personal relationships. Surprisingly, these rank behind points in the permission hierarchy. Why? Because they don't scale.

Using the relationship you have with an individual is an extremely effective way to temporarily refocus his attention or modify his behavior, but this approach is completely dependent on individuals. An employee may move on, but a permission program remains. Dentists, for example, don't get very much money when they "sell" their practices. Why? Because there's no guarantee that the consumer will enjoy the new dentist as much.

Personal relationships in the business world are slow and difficult to make deeper. It might take years of golf and excellent products and focused selling and word of mouth to make a relationship more profitable.

The corner dry cleaner has your permission to recom-

mend a new treatment for a stained coat or even to introduce a new service. A sign in his window is more likely to
get your attention than the same sign in a store you don't patronize.

Just because this permission doesn't scale well doesn't
mean it isn't vital and useful and powerful. By identifying the
right individuals and working to earn their trust and permission, retail and business-to-business marketers can make a
huge impact on their bottom line.

Ted Herman sold an $11 million computer system to a di-
vision of the New York City government. A sale that big covered lots of quotas, and it was accomplished by leveraging
personal relationships into permission to sell.

Wall Street deals wouldn't occur without this sort of permission, and Hollywood and Madison Avenue would floun-
der as well. Many companies have created multibillion-dollar
empires based on the permission they have to sell to just a
handful of companies. McDonnell Douglas did it with just
one client—the Pentagon.

Recognizing the value of personal relationship permission is essential to business growth. Disney, for example, has
top-level executives who do nothing but keep in touch with
the talent. They don't buy, they don't sell. They just keep the
permission channels open.

Think about your Rolodex for a second. You could probably divide it into three groups: highly permissioned contacts
(individuals you have permission to call and teach and sell to
at will); somewhat permissioned individuals (folks whom, because of word of mouth or previous contacts, you have the
right to at least try to market to); and finally, strangers you

know about, where you have to start from scratch to get permission.

I love my Palm Pilot organizer. It allows me to carry 2,000 contacts with me in my pocket. If someone stole it, would it do him any good? Would having a listing of more than fifteen years of my contacts in publishing and the Internet help him start or grow a business? I think not.

What is he going to say, "Hi, I stole Seth Godin's Pilot, I got your number, and I'd love to come meet with you tomorrow"? Of course not. The data's worthless. The permission is priceless. Yet for marketers who aren't harvesting and maintaining permission, making a cold call isn't much more than that.

Cambridge Technology Partners is a high-tech programming and consulting firm that's growing like a weed. They focus 100 percent of their sales on the information technology departments at the 1,000 largest companies in the country. In fact, there are only 1,000 people they really care about—the Fortune 1,000 CIOs.

From the very beginning, CTP has used Permission Marketing to make sales. They invite these very busy, but occasionally confused, executives to high-level seminars. At the seminars they book top business leaders to speak about critical issues facing the IT community. And there's no sales pitch. Thornton May, the brilliant marketer who runs the program, doesn't want to make a sales pitch. He's not even that concerned about getting a detailed list of exactly which problems his prospects face. Instead all Thornton wants is permission to speak with them, someday, with authority.

When CTP is ready to make a sales call, ready to identify

and cure Company X's problem, the permission that Thornton has earned is well worth the investment the company has made. At $5,000 or more per company, the permission isn't cheap. But it is an extraordinary value.

Individual permission is essential for a doctor, a lawyer, or any professional. But because it is so personal, it carries a number of risks.

Bad service or a bad interaction can cancel this sort of permission forever. A trusted chiropractor who uses a new technique that causes sudden discomfort discovers that he has lost a patient forever.

In addition, many marketers are unable to deliver completely different levels of service to different audiences. A dry cleaner can't readily offer cheap and fast service to one customer and expensive and perfect dry cleaning to another. One customer might want to get in and out of the store in a hurry, while another wants to linger and chat. If the permission is based on the charisma and personal interaction of the merchant, conflicts will inevitably arise.

Personal permission is the most powerful form of permission for making major shifts in a consumer's behavior. Frequent flier miles won't get someone to consent to open-heart surgery, no matter how many free trips are offered. But a doctor with the consumer's trust can make a difference.

Personal permission is also the single easiest way to move someone to an intravenous level of permission. It's the best way to sell custom products, very expensive products, or products that take an enormous amount of learning to appreciate.

If you're a professional with deep permission from qualified prospects, the single best way to improve your business is not by finding more clients, but by selling more stuff to the people who have given you permission already. If you're a corporate lawyer, do all your clients have their personal wills in order? If you're a heart doctor, could any of your patients benefit from a week of cholesterol reduction at the Pritikin clinic?

THE BRAND TRUST LEVEL

Much lower down the permission list is brand trust. This is the tried-and-true branding that is the mantra of most Interruption Marketers. It is the virtually unmeasurable but oh-so-fun way to be in the marketing business.

Marlboro communicates brand trust. So do Ivory and Campbell's and Starbucks and even Tom Peters. Brand trust is a vague, but soft and safe form of product confidence that consumers feel when interacting with a brand that's spent a ton of money on consistent, frequent interruptive messages.

Brand trust is dramatically overrated. It's extraordinarily expensive to create, takes a very long time to develop, is hard to measure, and is harder still to manipulate.

Yet it is also the most common way marketers practice their craft. Last year about half of all ad dollars went to advertising, not to direct mail and promotions. And this advertising was focused to a large degree on building brand trust.

Brand trust leads to brand extensions. If people trust Ivory soap, then by extension they'll trust Ivory dishwashing liquid. Marketers have spent a great deal of money over the last few years leveraging the brands that have been built over the last century.

When the new product reinforces the brand trust of the original, the permission is enhanced. If three or four line extensions all satisfy me, I'm much more likely to give you permission to show me a fifth one.

On the other hand, a brand extension that fails can do significant harm to brand trust. Once the marketer abuses the permission granted by the consumer, the consumer is in no mood to be abused again.

Apple lost a great deal of brand trust when it introduced the Newton with much fanfare. Microsoft risks the huge brand trust it has built every time it unleashes a new operating system on the public. This watershed moment is worth billions to Microsoft, and they (correctly) treat it that way.

The power of brand trust can be truly significant. A new product competing against a successful one has almost no chance to grab bandwidth. When we hear that there's a new Mazda Miata or that the VW Bug is back, we pay attention. On the other hand, if an unknown Korean company wants to introduce a sports car, it's less likely that we'll allow that message to cut through the clutter.

Brand trust doesn't apply just to packaged goods and cars. It also impacts retailers, restaurants, and even individuals. Tom Peters's next book will get instant attention from hundreds of thousands of people. And if it's good, they'll all buy it. But if he writes two or three clunkers in a row, he's burning the permission, making it less and less likely that consumers will sit up and take notice the next time he wants to talk with them.

Bell Atlantic is a prime example of a company burning its brand trust in exchange for short-term profits. A few years ago a letter from them meant you were getting a phone bill. You opened it, read it, and paid it.

Then an eager marketer discovered that putting an offer into a letter that *looked* like a phone bill led to a large number of people opening it and reading it.

The short-term effect of this approach is that the permission is leveraged into greater response rates. Two or three times as many people sign up for call waiting when the offer comes in an envelope that looks like a bill. For a while.

Of course, Bell Atlantic isn't leveraging their brand trust. They're ruining it. The envelope/bill connection is no longer sacrosanct. It is no longer clear to the consumer that he must open the envelope. The end result is that bills won't get opened so quickly. Bills will not get paid so fast. And when Bell Atlantic speaks, the customer won't be so quick to listen.

This is a vitally important point. It's so, so easy to squander brand trust. AOL does it every day with the interrupt screens they use to annoy users. At first, AOL was an uncluttered medium. It was controlled entirely by one company, and they could balance the number of ads that were shown. The user came to expect that he could believe everything he saw on AOL and that it was worth paying attention.

Then AOL discovered that by stopping the user's clickstream and interrupting the flow of the user's experience, they could sell a bunch of books or long-distance services or whatever. Then they made a second error—they allowed dozens of different employees working within AOL to use these interrupt screens whenever they wanted to promote the products for which they were responsible.

With no internal cost to using the most effective interruptive tool available, the interrupt screens appeared throughout the service. Lots of goods and services were sold. And permission was squandered daily.

As you might expect, the response rate to these screens has plummeted. And the permission granted to AOL has decreased. Over time this loss of permission will cost AOL millions of dollars.

One of the paradoxes of focusing on brand trust as the desired level of permission is that it is subject to compression. Over time it gets harder and harder to raise the level of brand trust a consumer has. Is it possible to have a significantly better opinion of Campbell's or the New York Yankees or Bell Atlantic?

When the permission given to a brand is under attack by marketers who are sabotaging it, there aren't enough tools available to rebuild the original level of permission earned. The voice of the brand inevitably decays over time because without the ability to rescue consumer confidence on an individual basis, it's too expensive to regain an entire nation's deteriorated view of a brand.

Here's a parable to bring it into focus. When your church newsletter first was distributed, everyone read it. It had a few relevant, anticipated, useful pieces of information that more than made up for the time it took to read.

Over time, though, this newsletter, like all church newsletters, became filled with trivia. A column by the church librarian on the history of the steeple. Lists of which hymns were scheduled for next week. All sorts of information was included because it was easy, it was cheap, and at least some constituency within the church thought it was a good idea.

Over time the newsletter gets longer. And less useful. Less relevant. Until one day it falls off each person's radar. Not enough time in your day, too much clutter, maybe later.

Is brand trust a worthwhile level of permission? By all means! But it must be guarded, and tended to, and invested in. Great brand marketers know how to gently leverage and even build brand trust. Shortsighted ones, however, can burn it down with amazing haste.

THE SITUATION LEVEL

The last useful level of permission is situational permission. This is very time sensitive but also very useful.

Situational permission is usually preceded by the question "May I help you?" When a consumer calls an 800 number, she has given situational permission. When you stop to ask for directions, or to ask a store clerk for advice on a gift, or when you buy just about anything from anyone, you've given situational permission.

In some ways this is a very powerful tool indeed. The consumer and the salesperson/marketer have very high physical and social proximity. The consumer has initiated the particular interaction, so there is no question of appropriateness. Generally, there is either money on the table right now or in the near future, or the consumer wouldn't have initiated the dialogue.

Compared to a television commercial or other interruptive technique, this is an opportunity for almost any marketer. However, it must be treated properly or it evaporates.

Because there are millions of potential customers, your marketers are your front-line people—the folks behind the cash register or those answering the phones. So the first concern revolves around leveraging this large and generally untrained group of marketers. There's a reason they wear those uniforms at McDonald's—it's the easiest way to mandate a level of quality.

If this type of marketing is important, the organization must invest a lot of time and money in training its front line on how to leverage the permission. "Do you want fries with that?" are perhaps the six most profitable situational permission marketing words in history. With 100,000 employees repeating that mantra to millions of customers every day, McDonald's has generated billions of dollars in incremental sales using situational permission.

The second concern is that this level of permission is so temporary that if it isn't handled quickly and well, it disappears. That's why the second best thing to do (after selling some fries) is to figure out how to upgrade this permission into something higher.

Flight attendants, for example, have the ability to sell passengers on enrolling in a frequent flier program. Thus the airlines can leverage their few moments on the intercom into a multiyear, controlled marketing campaign.

Fast-food restaurants can sell a birthday club. Dentists can sell a health maintenance plan. When you call a newspaper to suspend your subscription while you're on vacation, they can ask to upgrade you to automatic subscriptions via charge card billing.

SPAM

At the baseline level, the zero point, the place where every Interruptive Marketer starts, is spam. There's no permission here. Many marketers who do targeting assume that just because an advertisement is relevant, it's not spam.

I beg to differ.

Most marketing is spam. TV ads are spam (but infomercials, surprisingly enough, aren't). Direct mail to strangers is spam. So are radio ads and the king of all spam, junk e-mail.

It's called spam because of a Monty Python sketch in which everything on the menu includes Spam (a rather odd form of canned meat, in case you didn't know). In the sketch, eggs and bacon come with Spam. Baked beans come with Spam. Even the Spam comes with Spam. And the comedy troupe sings the word "Spam" over and over again to mock the ridiculous notion of forcing Spam onto every table whether you want it or not.

Junk e-mail is the king of spam because it doesn't cost anything to send. Literally. A spam marketer online can send five million unsolicited commercial e-mail messages for about $50. Given the superlow cost, any marketer with the guts to withstand the hatred of millions can make money with virtually no investment.

Online users realize that uncontrolled spam would mean the end of the Internet they love. E-mail would cease to function. In a friction-free world in which there is no cost associated with the ever-increasing clutter, the clutter would soon become overwhelming.

What if the postmaster general called the folks at L. L.

Bean and offered them free postage for a year? And then R. R. Donnelly called to offer them free printing as well? What would happen to their profits? Through the roof, they'd go. And they'd start sending catalogs every day, not every month. Business would increase, and there'd be happiness in Maine.

But what if the postmaster general and Donnelly turned around and offered the same deal to every single catalog company? Suddenly there'd be millions of catalogs in your mailbox—every day. An infinite onslaught of marketing. And L. L. Bean would go out of business for lack of sales. The clutter would clog the channels they rely on, and in a friction-free marketing world, the spam would become unbearable.

Marketing messages are going to continue to get cheaper as the number of media channels increases. The cost of printing will continue to become less important as electronic media use increases. With an infinite number of Web sites and an infinite number of cable TV channels, there will be an infinite number of interruptive ads. And the Permission Marketers will win.

It's clear to me that the most important part of the permission troika—anticipated, personal, and relevant—is anticipated. And spam is not just unanticipated, it's dreaded.

SEVEN

Working with Permission as a Commodity

You're not allowed to date your best friend's girlfriend.

Once you have earned permission, you must keep it and attempt to expand it. These four rules go a long way to help marketers understand permission:

1. Permission is nontransferable.
2. Permission is selfish.
3. Permission is a process, not a moment.
4. Permission can be canceled at any time.

PERMISSION IS NONTRANSFERABLE

It doesn't matter how long you've been dating—you're not allowed to send a stand-in on a date. You're not allowed to date your best friend's girlfriend or boyfriend.

This rule causes direct marketers the biggest fits. Why? Because in traditional marketing it is totally okay to rent or sell or transfer data. It gets done, secretly, every single day. In fact, it's a multibillion-dollar industry.

131

It's scary, but it's true: You can rent the name and address of every woman in New York City who has a permit to carry a gun. Then you can filter this data further to produce a list of those women who have a child in private school. Or who live in a building with a high likelihood of tenants who stay in first-class hotels when they travel. Want a list of dental floss users? Not a problem. You can even buy them by brand!

Perhaps the most amazing personal data available comes from the supermarket. If you carry a savings or bonus card, a computer somewhere knows exactly which groceries you buy.

Last year more than $1.2 trillion worth of goods and services were sold by direct mail. More than half of that was sold directly to consumers. So the information stakes are high.

Direct mail marketers have discovered that the way to combat their arch enemy—the cost of stamps and printing—is to buy the very best mailing lists they can find. They test and refine and research and cross-reference, all in search of increasing the response rates to their mailings by a tenth of a point.

Permission Marketing is at odds with the secret sorting and evaluation of data. Why? Because it takes consumers by surprise. And when you surprise a consumer, not only do you void permission, you increase fear. More than 80 percent of all consumers polled indicated that they're afraid of the data being collected about them. Far worse (from a marketer's point of view) is that this same fear is the single greatest impediment to consumers shopping online.

The transferability of permission seems harmless until you realize that once transferred, it ceases to be permission. If a company sends me a mailing that I didn't explicitly ask for, I am going to ignore it. We're back to spam again.

The morality of gathering information isn't as important for this discussion as the effectiveness of it. And even relevant advertising when directed to recipients without their permission cannot be as effective as that same advertising with permission attached.

On the Net, a company called Imgis is about to completely eliminate banner advertising as Web surfers have come to know it. Today, when you visit a Web site, you see a small rectangular ad on the bottom of the screen. The ad is pretty brainless—it doesn't know who you are, where you came from, or if you've seen that ad before. But by serving the ad from its own computers (instead of using those provided by the site itself), Imgis has the ability to store a small file on the user's computer. Your computer. This file, called a cookie, allows Imgis to remember certain things about you over time. More important, it lets them watch what you do across multiple sites.

Individually, cookies pose no threat at all to consumers and their privacy. That's because each site can store only its own information about you, and thus you're not telling the site something it didn't already know. To put it simply, a cookie was designed as a long-term storage mechanism to make it easy for a site to remember your passwords or preferences from visit to visit.

But using one company to serve ads across multiple sites pokes a hole in that restriction. Now Imgis can track you from site to site. So if you saw an ad while you were visiting Lycos and then went to a different site and saw a different ad, the Imgis computer might know who you are and where you'd been. This gives Imgis the ability to show different banners to each individual based on what they know about them. Soon banners will be like e-mail—completely personal.

But how can Imgis find out who you are? That's the trick, and that's where some level of permission comes in. They're going to work with major sites that require registration to enter (some of the sports sites do this, for example). In order to see the cool content (the bait they offer), you have to give up personal data and give the site some level of permission to do something with that data.

The problem, of course, comes from the fact that these sites intend to hand over the information to Imgis, sometimes without explicit permission from the user.

Will the Imgis banners work? No doubt. They'll certainly work better than the anonymous banners that currently fill the Web. Hence my prediction that current banners will be gone within two years. But will they work as well as they could? Absolutely not.

By attempting to transfer the slim permission that marketers are acquiring, they devalue it. By surprising consumers, by sending unsolicited commercial messages to them, Imgis makes the clutter problem worse, not better.

Contact the great Permission Marketers and ask to rent their list. They'll all turn you down. The reason is simple: *Permission rented is permission lost.* They can make far more money by protecting this asset than they can by destroying it.

Esther Dyson understands permission as well as any marketer. At first glance, it appears that Esther is a newsletter publisher. *Release 1.0,* which is edited by Jerry Michalski, is an insightful look at new technology. It's also expensive: more than $1,000 a year. Yet Esther has thousands of subscribers. Why? Because she runs one of the most influential new technology conferences in the world. Most of the influential executives in the industry attend, as do investors, media pundits, and the large companies that are often the first to adopt new computer systems.

It used to be that the only way to be invited to the conference was to subscribe to her newsletter. But the newsletter gained such popularity over the years that she's split off the PC Forum from the newsletter. To attend the next PC Forum, an attendee has to fill out a registration form and be selected as a participant. Esther has created a flurry of hand raising, a cycle of permission, and an ongoing process of communication that continues to expand her business as well as her reputation.

Esther gets permission to interrupt the very busy day of these key executives. She has earned that permission by providing a great newsletter and by providing an invitation to her conference.

She then leverages the permission she has from executives who listen to her to get access to the key executives in the industry who wish to talk to them. Every one of them makes an interview with Esther a priority. She gets first look at everything and regularly scoops the industry. She then can make the newsletter even more attractive, thus generating ever more permission.

You can't buy her mailing list. And you can't sponsor her annual PC Forum or even buy a slot as a co-presenter. Permission leveraged is permission enhanced. Permission rented is permission lost.

PERMISSION IS SELFISH

One of the reasons marketers are so quick to buy and sell data is that they love to be in control. A list that can be bought can be mailed to—whether or not the consumer wants to receive it. The law of large numbers means that sooner or later a sale is going to happen, and if the cost is low enough and the list is targeted enough, many marketers feel it's worth a try.

But Permission Marketing embraces the opposite approach. The marketer is not in control, the consumer is. And the consumer is selfish. Consumers care very little about you, your company, your products, your career, or your family. They're not likely to spend time trying to discover how you can help them solve their problems.

The heart of Permission Marketing is giving the stranger a *reason* to pay attention, while Interruption Marketers hold people hostage. Occasionally they resort to entertainment, and sometimes even information, but more often than not the goal is to use the "commercial break" to drill a message into the prospect's subconscious.

Have you ever looked forward to a Wisk commercial? Probably not. But the wise marketers behind the product knew that if they drilled deep enough, someday you'd grab their product in the supermarket. In Permission Marketing the opposite is true. You must find a reason for the prospect to pay attention. You have to offer an explicit reward—information, education, entertainment, or even cold hard cash—to get the consumer to opt in to the message.

In today's infoglut, people are more selfish than ever. And they're most selfish about their time and attention. Without a really good reason, you're not going to grab a piece of their most precious resource.

Ignoring selfishness is perhaps the biggest trap nonpolished Interruption Marketers fall into. They create advertising that impresses their mom, not their customers. Of course, if you interrupt enough, even bad advertising will generate some results.

Permission Marketers make every single interaction selfish for the consumer. "What's in it for me?" is the question that must be answered at every step.

That's why affinity programs and other promotions are such an effective overlay for many marketing campaigns. If you have a device that automatically rewards consumers for paying attention, you can allow the messages to develop more slowly and effectively over time.

At Yoyodyne we focus on sweepstakes because the very obvious rewards we offer make it easier to get people to opt in. But other techniques work well, too. You can offer up-to-the-minute sports scores. Or an ongoing education on a topic of mutual interest. Making the information itself a reward works quite well. For example, a free report on salaries offered by a recruiting firm is a great way to begin a permission relationship.

Robert Half (a recruiting firm) starts the permission process by running ads in local and regional publications with a few attractive job listings in the area. They include the position title, a brief description of responsibilities and requirements, and salary information. The call to action is to contact Robert Half for a complimentary copy of their current salary guide, which you can also get through their Web site. They ask the question "Curious about how your salary compares?" Almost everybody wants to know if they're underpaid, overpaid, or in the middle.

As recruiters, Half's business revolves around matching employers with employees, specifically in the area of accounting, financial, and information systems. When the customer phones in to request the free salary guide (or fills out an online application from their Web site), Robert Half obtains permission to establish a mutually beneficial exchange of information.

To continue the permission exchange, their Web site features something they call My Job Agent, which allows you to search for jobs using job characteristics defined by you. Under accounting jobs, for example, you can choose titles ranging from assistant bookkeeper to CFO using the pull-down menu options. Then you choose which state you want to search in. You give them a yearly salary target, and you can even perform word searches for your specific needs. The search pulls up all matches for your criteria.

But in order to begin the search process you have to register by supplying your name, a unique user name and password, your full address, and the method you would like used to contact you (e-mail, fax, phone, or post). If you provide your e-mail address, they automatically send you job updates as they come in, as well as the latest industry news if you want (their Web site includes links to Reuters Business and Technology News). From the perspective of the job seeker, immediate access to a potential gold mine of job opportunities is all the self-serving incentive required. Permission Marketing is under way.

Obviously Robert Half's asset is way more valuable than that of a recruiter who must rely on running another ad every time he has another job opening to fill. By rewarding the consumer, Robert Half turns a monologue into a dialogue.

In summary, the successful Permission Marketer first offers an obvious benefit to the right audience. Second, because it is so allied with the services being offered, the congruence makes it far easier to escalate the customer up the permission ladder.

On the other side of the spectrum, marketers who have earned permission often take it for granted. They cease to consider the selfish needs of the consumer and begin to use the permission in their own interest, not in the consumer's interest. This leads to a dramatic drop in the effectiveness of the campaign and to the eventual dissolution of the permission altogether.

PERMISSION IS A PROCESS, NOT A MOMENT

Interruption Marketing is all about the moment. Impact counts for everything, and the best practitioners of this craft are masters of impact techniques. You can measure traditional marketing techniques using tools like day-after recall, which identifies what percentage of the people exposed even remember the ad. In direct mail, marketers measure how many orders they get within a week of a mailing. This is all about the moment.

Permission Marketing, on the other hand, is a process. It begins with an interruption but rapidly becomes a dialogue. This dialogue, as I mentioned earlier, is a lot like dating. If managed properly, the relationship flourishes. If not, the investment in the first interruption is lost and the dialogue ends.

Investing in the process and testing the results of the investment can dramatically change the outcome. In early Yoyodyne promotions, our response rate to e-mails we sent grew from 2 percent to 36 percent. How? By painstakingly testing and evolving our communications techniques.

The low cost of frequency in this medium (e-mail) allows marketers to focus on the process, plant seeds, fertilize them, water them, and watch them grow. Of course, it takes patience and confidence—Permission Marketing cannot work overnight.

Robert Half's recruiting firm uses permission as a process as they slowly move customers further up the permission ladder. As time goes by, Robert Half informs the recipient about job opportunities, better jobs with higher compensation, in exchange for more detailed information about each customer in the form of a résumé, which they don't ask for right away. In addition to new job listings, Robert Half also offers a new free booklet about every two months. The communication going on here is clearly a process.

Another example of the depth to which the process of interaction can take place is Marshall Industries, a $1.5 billion distributor of industrial electronic components and production supplies. They represent over 150 suppliers, which makes them a one-stop shopping warehouse for buyers, manufacturers, integrators, and engineers who design computers, peripherals, and other electronic gadgets.

Marshall has leveraged technology to empower their customers with more and more free services that other distributors don't offer. And in doing so, they extend and magnify the value of the process of getting and maintaining permission. According to *NetMarketing* magazine, Marshall has the best business-to-business marketing Web site in existence. It serves every level of customer, from first-time visitor to loyal super-customers.

Consider the special problems of an engineer who's designing a widget. He might have all kinds of questions about which DSP chip to integrate into his new handheld golf course sandtrap and hazard finder. Most companies have mechanisms by which to download data sheets and other product information, but this is a monologue.

Marshall Industry's Web site allows engineers to tap into Marshall's secure online lab to experiment with designs. Engineers can download sample code, modify it to fit their specific design needs, test it on a virtual chip that's linked to the Internet, verify its performance, and, if it works, receive programmed chip samples within forty-eight hours. What's the cost to the engineer? Permission to continue building the relationship.

The process of ongoing exchange doesn't stop there, however. Help@Once is a chat service offering customers online support. Once you've entered the chat room, a Marshall technical support engineer is available to answer questions and provide technical assistance twenty-four hours a day.

PERMISSION CAN BE CANCELED AT ANY TIME

Traditional marketing has the consumer at its mercy. Marketers can send ads as often as they can afford to. With permission, the tables are turned. Consumers can cancel permission at any time.

Knowing that the end is always a moment away makes the marketer do a better job. Every communication must be crafted with the goal of ensuring that it's not the last one.

Scheherazade knew how to use this technique. She lived (according to the fable) in an Arabian land ruled by a crazy dictator. Every day the dictator married another beautiful woman. He enjoyed their honeymoon and the next day had her beheaded.

When it came Scheherazade's turn, she had the natural insecurity of a Permission Marketer—she knew that she might be canceled the next day. Her strategy was brilliant. That night, before she and the king went to bed, she told him a story. It was personal and relevant, and the king was eager to hear what happened next.

A few paragraphs before the end Scheherazade decided that she was too tired to continue and promised to finish the story later. The next morning she turned to the king and said, "I guess it's time for my beheading." The king, eager to hear how the story turned out, demurred. "No, my dear. We can wait until tomorrow. Tonight you will complete the story for me."

You can probably guess the ending. Each night for 1,001 nights, Scheherazade finished a story and then told a new story, promising the ending tomorrow. After more than three years, the king forgot all about beheading her, and she had a customer for life.

EIGHT

Everything You Know About Marketing on the Web Is Wrong!

How the Web is misused as an extension of broadcast media.

A QUICK LOOK AT THE SHELVES OF BOOKS written on marketing online would give the neophyte the mistaken impression that it's possible to profitably market your company on the Internet by treating it like a broadcast medium. The authors of these books believe that since they can run "ads" on the Internet, and get "viewers," and those viewers can be marketed to, a brand can be built and eventually sales will follow.

Forgive the following jeremiad, but it's necessary because it corrects a deeply held belief by many journalists and industry veterans. It's important to take a solid whack at this vision of the Internet because it is leading to the loss of billions of dollars online, and worse, because of these losses, it's making many marketers pessimistic about the power of the Internet as a marketing tool.

The idea that the Internet is a medium just like TV supports the old way of thinking about marketing, but it just doesn't work the same way.

The Internet is not a million-channel universe that will

soon be stocked with terrific new shows and personalities and movies on demand. It seems as though every time a new medium comes along, everyone wishes it were TV. When video games were introduced in the 1970s, the race was on to make them TV-like. When consumer software games and educational products first came along in the 1980s, the goal was to beat *Sesame Street*. When CD-ROMs were introduced later in that decade, the hot companies were those that were putting their resources into motion and sound, offering a cinemalike experience.

Why the rush to emulate TV? Two very good reasons. First, every American believes that he or she is born with two inalienable rights: the right to be elected president of the United States and the right to direct a major Hollywood motion picture. Being president is no fun anymore, so now everyone wants to be in show business.

The problem with show business is that it's a brutal business, with a very small number of insecure people having all the fun and the glory. High school with money, some folks call it.

The second reason is that the FCC (and then the cable companies) have always severely limited the number of channels available to producers of TV. First there were three networks. Even today there are really only ten major players, with most systems hosting just thirty or forty available channels.

This artificially limited supply of channels dramatically increases the demand for programming. And demand for programming means that the networks can charge a significant premium for acting as an intermediary between viewers and advertisers. It's an oligopoly, and a potentially lucrative one.

Corporate America is filled with executives itching for a chance to start programming a network. They see the impact TV has on American lives, they see the money that a successful network can make (I mean, even the Weather Channel makes a ton of money!), and they're eager to use corporate money to have some fun.

The idea of the five-hundred-channel (or five-million-channel) universe is incredibly compelling to a lot of major media companies. They see the cost of creating a network dropping dramatically, but they fail to consider the fact that with the number of channels going through the roof, the value of adding another network comes increasingly closer to zero.

Let's take a close look at the numbers, and you'll see how horrible it really looks. There are ten major networks. Every night about 200 million watch one or more of them. That's 20 million people, on average, per network. With 20 million viewers and a distribution cost that is close to zero (one more viewer costs no more to reach), this has the makings of an insanely profitable business model.

As I mentioned at the beginning of this book, there are 2 million corporate Web sites in operation today. It costs about $1 billion a year for these companies to build and maintain them. Yet there are only 50 million people surfing the Web on a good day. That's an average of twenty-five people per site, per day. *That's like having 8 million TV networks instead of ten.*

In the last year we have seen huge losses from CNet,

Sportsline, and other content sites. The Spot, ranked the coolest site on the entire Web eighteen months ago, is now bankrupt. If commercial entertainment sites, stocked with professional photos, compelling writing, news teams, and big promotional dollars, can't attract enough of an audience to break even, what chance does your company have? Even if you can persuade someone to come to your company's Web site once, what chance do you have of getting her to return?

There are a lot of vested interests here. Most ad agencies, for example, want and need the Web to be a broadcast medium, not a direct medium. As agencies have seen their traditional business get hammered, most have built Web divisions. However, almost without exception these divisions are modeled exactly on the TV model. They have creative departments stocked with sullen twenty-five-year-olds in black churning out cool Web sites, and media departments looking to buy ad space.

Technology providers need the constant increase in demand for more and more sizzle (cool content on Web sites) to drive the adoption of new technologies. Intel has an entire division that funds start-up companies, with the sole goal to promote the development of cutting-edge stuff that people can't see without upgrading their computers.

Content providers—the writers, artists, and musicians who make their money from creating media—are also focused on making the Internet a broadcast medium. CNet, ZDNet, Pathfinder—there are dozens of sites that employ thousands of well-meaning creative people who are all focused on generating content because the technology of the Web *can* support it, not because it should.

At last count ZDNet had more than 250,000 pages of data on their site, with another 500 being added daily. Yet the average visitor to their site looks at a grand total of four pages! Rather than investing in *new* pages, ZDNet needs to figure out how to have people look at the ones they've already got.

Finally, the early adopter consumers, the folks with beepers, personal digital assistants, fast modems, and fast computers, are eager and itching to see ever more advanced stuff on their computers. A few years ago the most popular site on the Internet was the Ben & Jerry's home page. Why? Because if you clicked on the cow, it mooed. After a week, of course, the sizzle was old news to this audience and they moved on.

Hoping to capture the technology of the moment is not a marketing strategy for the faint of heart. The odds of getting it right are small, and the benefits from getting it right are almost nonexistent. Levi's had the coolest corporate Web site around for a while. They got lots of visitors, but it's not clear that it led to the purchase of any jeans. And once the buzz was gone, the traffic left and no asset had been created.

As new technologies and new techniques proliferate, it becomes more and more difficult to capture a substantial share of this early adopter attention focus. Jennicam, for example, is a much ballyhooed site in which voyeurs can peek on a twenty-one-year-old as she frolics through her bedroom (or, more likely, watch the empty, dark room while she's at work). I guarantee that by the time this book is published, Jennicam will no longer be the third most visited site on the Web—if it exists at all.

The almost manic rush to build sites in order to market

products was fueled by tremendous insecurity on the part of marketers, especially at big companies. It seems relatively low-cost ($100,000 to $1 million a year) and a great way to appear to be on the cutting edge. The chairman of the board gets to talk about the new technology initiatives at the board meeting, and the marketers get a much needed break from yet another package redesign focus group.

When K-Tel announced that they were about to go onto the Internet, their stock tripled in value. There's a tremendous buzz among marketers and investors, and many companies are milking it for all they can.

The cost of all this play is significant, though. In addition to wasting time, money, and energy, it is sapping the focus away from the real point, the real benefit of the Web. And the downside is that once burned, big companies will abandon the Web, certain to be replaced by a new generation of little companies that are brave enough to use the medium properly.

Marketers have failed to do some basic analyses. Here are the questions that must be answered in order to have a coherent strategy when facing the Web:

1. What are we trying to accomplish?
2. Can it be measured?
3. What is the cost of bringing one consumer, one time, to our Web site?
4. What is the cost of having that consumer return?
5. If this works, can we scale it?

THE MOST POPULAR MYTHS ABOUT MARKETING ON THE WEB

1. Traffic (Hits!) Is the Best Way to Measure a Web Site

A year ago the easiest way to measure traffic was in hits. A hit is nothing but a single ping on your Web server. One page might be responsible for one hit, or it might account for twenty. Even worse, there's no metric to convert hits to sales, or hits to market share, or hits to branding. Traffic to your site costs time and money, and you ought to spend that money (and test that spending) as wisely as any other marketing expenditure you make.

2. If You Build Great Content, People Will Return Over and Over

What do you get if you cross an insomniac with a dyslexic and an agnostic? Someone who stays up all night worrying about whether there really is a dog.

It's pretty funny the first time.

But the second time it doesn't even make you smile. Imagine telling a joke to a group of people, then inviting them back tomorrow to hear the same joke again. Not many will show up. In order to build a thriving content site, you must offer news (and that's expensive) or truly customized data (like Federal Express's innovative tracking system that tells you where your package is at any given moment). The desire to create fresh coolness has overwhelmed many online marketers.

The cost of creating an infinite supply of fresh and cool content that is somehow related to your business is overwhelming. And with 1.8 million commercial Web sites to choose from, you can be virtually certain that people won't pick yours.

Remember, people won't come back unless you remind them to. Imagine a magazine that relied only on newsstand sales, with no subscribers. A traditional commercial Web site is just that—an online magazine with no regular subscribers, no home delivery, no way to get people to come back. The one-shot anonymous visit is a sure route to failure.

3. You Can Sell Stuff on the Web If You Invest Enough in a Secure Server

Commerce isn't about technology. It's about selling. You can outfit an online store in just a few minutes using very low cost services on the Web. But focusing on your infrastructure instead of your marketing will leave you with a store that has no sales.

I like to say that you need more than a gun to be a gun-slinger. The focus on outfitting sites with the latest triple-encrypted software is a red herring. The real challenge selling stuff online is in the selling, not in the technology.

4. The Search Engines Are the Key to Traffic to Your Site

The top one hundred searched words are unprintable, off color, or pornographic. The rest often lead to thousands (or tens of thousands) of matches. And amazingly enough, *50 percent of all searches are failures*. Vast numbers of people are using the search engines. But any single Web site is a very tiny needle in a very big haystack.

It's vital that you create a process that leads to a scalable mountain of traffic that doesn't depend on random visits via the search engines.

5. You Need Java and Shockwave to Be at the Cutting Edge

Which is more important, what works or what's new? The vast majority of consumers want mastery of technology, not the cutting edge. Do you want proof? Try Yahoo! or GameBoy. GameBoy is seven-year-old technology that sells and sells. Yahoo! offered the least powerful search among all of the search engines but provides an easy, fast, simple solution.

It turns out that according to a Gallup poll, more than 85 percent of the people online consider themselves smarter than average. :-) Yet these overeducated people are made to feel stupid every single time they go online. They don't have the right plug-in, they haven't downloaded the right file, their modem is too slow. If your site makes them feel stupid as well, it will fail.

6. The Web Is Like TV

No. It's a poor substitute for TV. And faced with viewing the Web as a substitute, those who want the original switch back. Bill Gates has spent more than half a billion (with a *b*) dollars trying to build programming for the Web that would lead to repeat traffic. Every single one of his efforts to create a show has failed. The more you make it like TV, the worse you do.

Someday, when we have fiber or cable network access to the home, it's likely that the Web and TV will merge. When it happens, though, don't look for an explosion of free programming. With millions of channels, the economic model for creating first-rate programming is eliminated.

In the meantime, with the combination of low bandwidth and a virtually infinite number of choices, it's essentially impossible to build a TV-like content business on the Web that has a chance of paying off.

7. Lots of People Surf the Web

The average Web user has been to one hundred sites and bookmarked just fourteen of them. There's actually an awful lot of activity by just a few people. Because journalists are among the most aggressive surfers, we read a lot about the neatest new things on the Web. But after the novelty wears off, most of these sites just fade away from a user's experience.

8. If You Don't Experiment Now, You'll Lose Later

No, if you don't experiment *well* now, you'll lose later. Bad experiments yield bad data. There are obvious and hidden costs to all the experimentation going on today. The worst side effect is that we're creating an entire generation of content programmers and media buyers who have learned a method of doing business online that's totally out of touch with reality.

9. Your Site Should Be a Complete Online Experience

Netscape, AOL, Yahoo!, and a few others are building entry sites to the Web called portals. The idea behind these sites is that they offer everything an online user could want in one "place."

Most companies can't afford to build a portal strategy

properly, and doing half the job well is worse than not doing it at all. Very few players can really offer everything a user needs all in one place: free e-mail, free chat, and so forth. It'll wipe out the budget you should be using to promote yourself correctly.

10. Anonymity Is Good for the Net

The Net is fundamentally an anonymous medium, though it didn't start that way. Today, with dozens of companies offering anonymous accounts, you can be anyone you want online.

Imagine a prospect walking into a retail store wearing a ski mask. "I'm just looking," would be an understatement. People in masks are rarely good citizens, and they virtually never buy anything. Anonymity leads to spam, to onetime visits, to a lack of marketing effectiveness, and to bad behavior. Great marketers entice consumers to give up anonymity.

Permission Marketing rewards individuals for giving up their anonymity. Traditional Web techniques embrace anonymity and fail because of this shortcoming.

11. You Can Make Money Selling Banners

No, you can't! The supply will always exceed the demand, and only a few superaggregators can win. Even Excite, one of the three or four largest sites on the Web, has an unsold inventory of 85 percent. Imagine a magazine in which five out of six ad pages were blank or unsold!

Banners were invented because they were a convenient way for Web content and search sites to make money, not because they worked. With the rise of personalized Web servers like Imgis, undifferentiated banners will fade away.

12. Activity Is Good

Many, many companies have fallen prey to the fact that they can build just about everything on the Web themselves. Because they can tweak their site daily, build chat rooms, and invest all manner of top management time, they do, incorrectly believing that they're doing marketing.

Take a look at most large company sites (General Electric being my favorite), and you'll see the work of a large, well-paid committee of executives who had little idea what they were doing.

NINE

Permission Marketing in the Context of the Web

Free stamps—the Web changes everything.

UNLESS YOU'VE BEEN LIVING under a rock for the last three years, you've heard one pundit after another proclaiming that the world will be forever changed by the Internet. Yet with Jennicam, spam, chat rooms about lizards, and downloadable photos of Teri Hatcher (the actress best known for playing Lois Lane on the recent TV series), it's not clear to most marketers what all the fuss is about.

Jeff Bezos is on his way to becoming a billionaire because of Amazon.com—but it appears to be just a bookstore (albeit a bookstore now worth more than Barnes & Noble and Borders Books *combined*).

Yahoo! has a market capitalization more than New York Times Corp., which owns newspapers and magazines around the country. Is there really something going on here, or is this another tulip bulb frenzy?

There is something very big going on, but as you could see from the previous chapter, it's not what some of the experts believe. *The Internet is the greatest direct marketing medium ever invented.* It is not TV.

Here are six of the biggest benefits it offers to direct marketers:

1. Stamps are free.
2. The speed of testing is one hundred times faster.
3. Response rates are fifteen times higher.
4. You can implement curriculum marketing in text and on the Web.
5. Frequency is free—you can identify and efficiently talk with individuals over and over again.
6. Printing is free.

Let's look at the Web through the prism of Permission Marketing and understand why this new medium delivers on the promise of permission.

Here are the five simple steps to any Permission Marketing campaign in the context of the Internet:

1. The marketer offers the prospect an incentive for volunteering.

On the Net, marketers can use banners to gently interrupt consumers and offer them an opportunity to opt in to a marketing program. This is the only media cost of the entire campaign.

Yes, Permission Marketers use banners. But they're just about the only ones who can use this medium effectively. A banner is a great way to get momentary attention and possibly opt-in from large numbers of individuals—and cheaply.

2. Using the attention offered by the consumer, the marketer offers a curriculum over time, teaching the consumer about the product or service.

Once a consumer has opted in, the marketer uses e-mail to remind the prospect to return to the Web site. E-mail is the number one use of the Web, with more than 80 percent of Web users listing it as the main reason they go online.

Because the e-mail box is hot, welcome messages in this slot get a lot of attention and reaction. Marketers use e-mail to teach the consumer about the benefits of the product. Best of all, the marketer can gain personal insights to make the marketing messages ever more personal.

3. The incentive is reinforced to guarantee that the prospect maintains the permission.

Because there's a cost-free communication infrastructure in place via the Internet, the intrinsic two-way dialogue going on allows the marketer to ascertain if the consumer is paying attention. By encouraging responses, it's easy to determine who's involved in the campaign and easier still to upgrade the rewards to consumers to maintain their interest.

4. The marketer offers additional incentives to get even more permission from the consumer.

A mass-market campaign must be the same for each viewer. But using the power of computers, the marketer can customize them for an audience of one. Thus there can be both direct rewards to the consumer to inspire participation and ongoing content rewards that make it ever more likely that the consumer will continue to upgrade permission. People who need more rewards to stay active can get them without corrupting the entire system.

5. *Over time, the marketer leverages the permission to change consumer behavior and turn it into profits.*

What is a 100 percent loyal, opt-in e-mail list worth? A completely personalized list of hundreds of thousands or millions of people who want and expect to hear from you on a personal and relevant topic related to purchases? In many cases it may be the most valuable asset in the company.

A permission approach adds a huge frequency element to the campaign. This frequency turns into a spectacular asset for the marketer.

Imagine, for example, if Pizza Hut were to send every loyal Pizza Hut customer with kids an e-mail offering them a free soda with purchase, but just tomorrow, and just at their particular local store. And by the way, there will be a clown and face painting!

If Pizza Hut can contact 2 million people this way, overnight and for free, what will be their return on investment? Is this more efficient than spending $1 million on TV advertising? Of course it is. Multiply it by fifty or one hundred messages a year, and you can see the power of the medium.

Even better, if the message to all 2 million people isn't the same, but instead reflects past purchasing behavior, neighborhood, family size, and more, won't the response rate be even higher?

Best of all, if protected properly, it's an asset that doesn't get used up. Far from it. It gets more powerful and deeper over time.

Caution! The opt-in step, the first one, is tricky, expensive, and slow. Because of this, many marketers may decide to skip it and just rent or buy a list of e-mail addresses. This is a bad idea for several reasons. The most obvious one (and the most dangerous) is that renting a list and then sending unsolicited commercial e-mails to people on that list is spam, and that practice will literally wreck your business.

Why Spam Is Like Shoplifting

For $100 a self-defeating marketer can buy about 6 million pieces of e-mail, addressed and delivered. Each e-mail is a page long, selling any product or service you can imagine. But only scam artists and uninformed marketers rely on sending millions of pieces of e-mail to strangers. And every company or individual that has tried this eventually fails. The two most notorious spammers of all time—the green card lawyers and the guy behind Cyberpromotions—were forced to retire. (I can't even bring myself to dignify these folks by mentioning their names in this book.)

Spam is like shoplifting. It costs the recipient a few seconds of time to open and delete unsolicited mail, thus representing the theft of a tiny amount of a very valuable asset. Defenders of spam point out that the acts of one individual won't bankrupt anyone, but this is irrelevant. One stolen purse from Macy's won't bankrupt them, either, but it's still wrong. If everyone did it, Macy's would be out of business.

The spammers who believe that consumers should have to opt out of these mailings miss the point, too. Macy's doesn't have to opt out of shoplifting. Shoplifters don't have the option of waiting until they get caught and *then* agreeing to stop. Spammers face the same obligation.

Consumers will fight back. They may boycott you, blacklist you, clog your mailbox, request that their Internet service provider file a complaint against you, or just speak ill of you to hundreds or even thousands of consumers (word travels fast over the Net). The damage that can be done to your brand, and your company, is huge. Remember, a list that is generated without overt permission is almost impossible to leverage. When you're back to interrupting strangers, it's extremely unlikely that you'll be successful in getting consumers to start a dialogue with you.

The law of permission is simple: To maximize the value of a list, you must maximize uniqueness, anticipation, and overtness.

The more unique the audience, the more anticipated the messages, and the more overt the opt-in (permission), the more valuable the list is.

HOW TO BUDGET PERMISSION INTO YOUR WEB SITE

Every commercial Web site should be set up to accomplish one goal. Your Web site should be 100 percent focused on signing up strangers to give you permission to market to them.

That's all. It doesn't have to be big or fancy or complicated or expensive. Instead, this front door to your business should be obsessed with getting permission.

Once you look at the Web from this perspective, many things fall into place. For example, you can easily calculate exactly what it costs to earn one more permission. The formula is:

Cost of banners to reach 1,000 people
divided by
Number of people who visited your site (of 1,000 possible)

This will give you the cost of getting one visitor to your site, one time. Multiply this number by the percentage of people who visited the site who opted in and gave their e-mail address and permission to market to them. (Remember, the more explicit the opt-in, the more valuable the permission. Tricking people into giving their e-mail address is a waste of time.)

You now know the cost of gaining permission. You have to compare it to the lifetime value of one of these permissions, and you can determine if the investment makes sense.

For example, imagine that you're starting a beer of the month club. The math might look like this:

Banners at $40 per thousand
2% click-through rate
$2 per visitor
33% opt-in, leading to a cost per permission of $6

If, over time, half of the people you engage in a dialogue with become customers, it's costing you about $12 to get a customer. If the lifetime value of this customer is $100, you're way ahead of the game.

It gets even better if your company sells a wide variety of products or if the products are expensive or complicated. How much does it cost Clinique or Hewlett-Packard or Hyundai to teach one more consumer all about their new products? HP might spend between $100 and $1,000 to teach just one more IT professional about a new workstation. Clinique pays huge shelving allowances and salaries just to put one person in front of a prospect to teach her about a new face cleanser.

It costs a car company almost $100 to get someone into the dealership. Using Permission Marketing, they could start these dialogues for about $5 each and take their time, weeks or months, educating consumers and then providing an incentive to visit the dealership.

Four Keys to Setting Up Your Permission-Based Web Site

1. Test and Optimize Your Offer

In order to structure a marketing campaign to get "opt-in" permission, it's necessary to recognize that the media cost is heavily weighted at the beginning. You pay for attention now and get it later.

Since you're not actually asking for a cash sale during your first interaction with the prospective customer, you can expect a much higher response rate than you would with a traditional direct mail campaign. Opt-in permission will go way up, though, if the media chosen, the banners that are used, and the entire process are tested and optimized. At Yoyodyne we've increased opt-in on some of our promotions from 3 percent to 40 percent just by testing.

Of course, if you're already using other media, you can leverage this tremendously by adding a feature that allows the customer to raise his hand. For example, every commercial you run can feature an e-mail address with a tag that reads, "For more information, write to us at info@ford.com."

A generation ago no one put an 800 number in an advertisement. Today you'd be crazy not to. An e-mail address is even better. It buys you permission and costs you nothing on the margin.

2. Make the Permission Overt and Clear

It doesn't pay to trick people into giving you permission. The idea is to have a mutually beneficial dialogue, and the more you tell people about what to expect, the greater the anticipation you'll be able to create. That's important as you work to leverage it.

Fine print isn't the answer here. The focus of the promotion or campaign should match the permission you're asking for. Amazon.com, for example, does quite well in using e-mail to remind people to come back and buy more books (it's part of the deal when you sign up with them, and most consumers anticipate and enjoy the messages).

It's tempting to automatically upgrade the permission a prospect has granted. It's tempting to rent, sell, or trade these permissions. As mentioned earlier, this usually fails, and it fails dramatically online.

Several organizations are making it easier for companies to communicate with consumers about privacy issues associated with e-commerce (giving up certain elements of privacy is a prerequisite when volunteering permission over the Internet). Online privacy, and how to protect it, is now rated by organizations that judge quality and service levels within the world of Web commerce, the way Standard & Poor's rates bonds and *Consumer Reports* rates consumer goods.

TRUSTe (http://www.truste.org) promotes trust through online privacy assurance. They review online sites and offer their stamp of approval (a TRUSTe logo) to those that qualify. This is what they want to know in terms of offering consumers online protection:

1. What information does the site gather and track about customers?
2. What does the site do with the information it gathers/tracks?
3. With whom does the site share the information it gathers/tracks?
4. What is the site's opt-out policy (important permission requirement)?
5. What is the site's policy on correcting and updating personally identifiable information?
6. What is the site's policy on deleting or deactivating names from their database?

At the same time, the Direct Marketing Association is trying to take the high ground in the privacy debate and has published very specific guidelines it asks members to follow.

Remember that jeopardizing one's privacy is the single largest reason given by consumers for not shopping online and for not opting in to promotions and marketing programs online. Of course, the online user knows that he has no privacy. What he's concerned about is inundation. He knows that in the wrong hands, one scrap of data about him can lead to an onslaught.

Making a promise, an overt deal, and keeping it is the secret to long-term success in Permission Marketing.

Don Peppers and Martha Rogers make a brilliant defense of privacy. Basically, any marketer doing one-to-one or permission campaigns will dramatically increase her profits not only by respecting privacy, but by becoming a zealot. As soon as the data is shared, its value decreases. By maintaining the privacy, the marketer enhances her asset.

3. Use Computers, Not People, to Send and Receive Information

There are approximately 10,000 seconds in a day. So if you have 10,000 people in your permission database and it takes your computer one second to handle each one, you've just maxed out your system.

Worse, if 1 percent of the people in your permission database require human contact every day, then half a million people in your permission database will lead to 5,000 customer service requests a day.

One of the huge drags on AOL's earnings growth is that one-third of all their employees are in customer service. What a waste! Not only is AOL paying a fortune for this, but the quality of the care isn't nearly as high as it would be if it were automated.

When creating an online Permission Marketing campaign, it's vitally important that you set expectations properly. If consumers expect that a human will be instantly available to answer their questions, they *will* ask questions and you should be prepared to answer them.

Early on at Yoyodyne, we discovered that we needed one full-time customer service person for every 10,000 people in the database. It quickly became clear to me that this would bankrupt us. So we reset our expectations on what we should provide to the consumer and built a sophisticated automated solution.

Today we have millions of people in the database but still don't need even a single full-time customer service person. We've successfully removed the need for much personal contact from our system.

Does this mean every marketer can? No, not at all. But it's essential that you triage your users and make sure that only the people who *need* human intervention are getting it. And you can accomplish this by making it very easy for consumers to escalate an issue when a human is truly needed.

4. Focus on Mastery—Online Consumers Need to Feel Smart

Online prospects are twice as likely as the national average to have a college degree. This is a group of people used to being right, used to figuring out how things work, and used to getting them to work quickly.

So imagine the frustration when these above average brainiacs come face to face with the Internet. Their machines crash. Sites are slow. They get fatal errors and Java script errors and browser errors. A plug-in is missing. It seems that at every turn the Net reminds people how stupid they are.

Of course, this is a tremendous opportunity. If you can

build simple tools that work, and you can make people feel smart for using them, prospects will flock to you and stay with you.

Never build anything that isn't fun on a 14.4 modem, or over AOL, or with an old browser.

The reason e-mail is the killer app is that it's simple and it does exactly what people expect it to do. Your Permission Marketing campaign should work the same way.

TEN

Case Studies

Companies that have done it right,
and some that haven't.

HOW A LITTLE KOSHER CATERER BURNS MONEY

Every Sunday for the last few weeks I've seen the same ad in
my local edition of *The New York Times*. The ad is for a
kosher gourmet shop, and it's promoting "kosher for
Passover" dishes for the upcoming holiday. Particularly obser-
vant Jews eat only certain foods throughout the eight-day holiday, so the opportunity to build business must have been
appealing to the store's owners.

Obviously the only audience for these products are religious Jews who need to buy food specially prepared for the
holiday. And while *The New York Times* suburban edition
probably ranks fairly high among the media choices available
to this store, it seems like a particularly wasteful example of
Interruption Marketing.

First, the ad is wasted on the 95 percent or more of readers who have no interest in or desire for this product. Second,
among the target group, many will never get to this page.
Third, among those who get to this page, few will read the

small print ad jammed with type closely enough to really understand what's being offered and, more important, what is the benefit of responding.

Because the ad features the shop's entire menu, its goal appears to be to have an interested consumer actually stop reading the paper, make sure the store is open, then call and order a product. Quite a long shot and, given the cost of the advertisement, a very expensive crapshoot.

Wouldn't it be better if the ad had just asked interested consumers to pick up the phone and call for a free menu or more information? By getting permission to talk with and eventually sell to the target audience, the store could have gotten the most mileage out of the $20,000 they invested in advertising.

Even better, though, would have been a strategy of not running the ad at all! Over the course of the year the shop could have collected permission from every single one of its customers to alert them before Passover came. They could have created joint marketing ventures with religious organizations and temples to leverage *their* permission (perhaps by offering a special discount to members who came in).

The end result of this year-long, persistent marketing campaign would be access—by way of phone, letter, or even e-mail—to thousands of motivated customers. By delivering a message that was anticipated, personal, and relevant, the shop could have dramatically cut marketing costs while it built profits.

And once it had a permission base, reselling this audience next year wouldn't require yet another $20,000 investment in Interruption Marketing.

MUTUAL FUND INDUSTRY: SMART MONEY AND DUMB MARKETING

The mutual fund industry is a great example of a booming business that continues to rely on very expensive interruption techniques to grow. Every week Dreyfus mutual funds spends hundreds of thousands of dollars running boring full-page ads in the newspaper. Have you ever seen one of these ads? I think they have a lion on them and usually run in the business section.

The ads feature no call to action to give the reader a reason to respond. They don't use a clever interruption strategy. And there isn't even a suite of messages once someone *does* respond. In short, Dreyfus is able, because of its size and profitability, to waste a great deal of money interrupting semi-qualified people with boring advertising.

Now that the market for mutual funds is more mature, now that each new investor is harder to get, the mutual funds probably regret using such wasteful tactics back when it was easier to grow.

A permission strategy that gives consumers a selfish reason to raise their hands makes great sense for this industry. After a consumer volunteers, he could be answered with a series of carefully tested messages that focus on *teaching* prospects the reason to invest with them.

After the first sale is made, the opportunity for further marketing is even greater and even more ignored. If you've got your money in a mutual fund, you know that you almost never receive friendly, easy-to-understand customer-centric mail. Instead, mutual fund users are inundated with unreadable, dense prospecti and other unanticipated, nonpersonal, irrelevant messages. What a waste.

Perhaps the most egregious form of spam marketing by phone are the stockbrokers working from boiler rooms who call "carefully selected" individuals at work or at home during dinner. The entire focus of this exercise is to trick the receptionist/secretary (or other gatekeeper) and get the rube on the other end of the phone line. Once there, the telemarketers lie to the prospect in the hope of getting a nibble (which is sort of an immoral spin on permission). Because the profit from these scams is so huge, the marketers don't really care that they're using an incredibly inefficient interruption technique to grab the attention of consumers.

None of these companies is building an asset or managing a long-term process. Instead the entire focus is to make money on each day's investment of time and energy. Next time one calls you, ask for references from current satisfied customers and you'll see what I mean.

THE AUTO INDUSTRY LOVES TELEVISION

If you watch much television, you've seen car advertising. It all looks the same—beautifully shot, glistening sheet metal, winding roads, happy families, farmland. The ads are extremely expensive to produce and broadcast. Auto manufacturers consistently spend huge amounts on advertising. General Motors, Chrysler, and Ford were three of the top ten spenders for all categories last year.

The ads, however, don't give consumers a reason to respond, nor do they even bother to give them a *way* to respond. There's no toll-free number, no local dealer name, no consumer-focused reason to respond. Instead they work to build the anemic stand-in for permission—a brand.

But with every model, with every initiative, the car companies have to start over from scratch. They have no idea which ads you've seen and which you haven't and no continuity from one broadcast ad to the next.

Car manufacturers know that far more powerful than their brand imagery is word of mouth, dealer satisfaction, and car quality. The ads they run do nothing to integrate any of these three evaluative techniques, which is one reason most car companies are using direct mail now as well. At least with direct mail the car manufacturers can offer a more focused message. Yet most of the mail they send is not heavily focused on getting a response or permission.

There are some notable exceptions. Thirty years ago Lester Wunderman, the father of direct marketing, conceived a suite of mailings for Lincoln. The goal was to drive Cadillac owners into a showroom to see the new Lincoln.

The mailings were relevant, because they were directed only at Cadillac owners. The challenge was delivering a curriculum that would allow them to teach these owners about the new Lincoln.

Using a personal letter from the head of the division, and delivering that letter in a focused way, Lincoln was able to cut through the clutter and get the attention of this hard-to-reach audience. They then followed up with several letters, each teaching a little more about the car. The end result was a huge increase in dealership visits at a fraction of the cost of TV.

Mercedes-Benz did the same thing with Rapp Collins last year when they introduced, several years late, their sport utility vehicle. A year before launch they carefully targeted likely purchasers and then engaged them in a dialogue. The goal was to use surveys to allow these prospects to be involved in the actual design of the car.

Based on responses to each survey, they sent additional customized follow-up surveys to each respondent. Over time they built a permission relationship that caused these consumers to pay attention to the messages and to trust the car. The campaign culminated in a beautiful package delivered to each participant that included a Mercedes hood ornament. The accompanying letter pointed out that since the participant had helped design the car, the company felt he deserved a part of the car! When they finally shipped, Mercedes sold out its entire run (40,000 cars at $50,000 each) immediately.

R. L. Polk sold more than $300 million in data to car manufacturers and dealers last year. The car marketers use this data to properly target their messages to people with the right demographics and car ownership status to warrant the mail.

I predict that within ten years one or more car manufacturers will realize how broken the entire system is and will fire their entire dealership force (an eighty-year-old albatross). Instead they'll demo and display cars in a company-owned showroom—probably in a shopping mall or other convenient location.

Then they'll use Permission Marketing to teach people about their car and to encourage trial and eventual pur-

chase. The average American visits only 1.5 car dealers before making a purchase, so staffing these showrooms with
noncommissioned, highly trained consultants is a smart
plan indeed.

Car dealers spent $3 billion marketing cars last year, but
it's not clear that this money adds value for the consumer or
the carmakers. Once this money is redeployed on Permission
Marketing, it can lead to significantly greater efficiencies.

The next step, though, is a bit more scary to the manufacturers. As mentioned earlier in the book, carmakers could
expand on the permission concept and stop selling cars altogether. Instead they can sell you transportation on a monthly
basis. A consumer would "subscribe" to a car company, and
for a flat fee, the company would agree to place a working,
serviced, late-model car in your driveway every day forever. It
might even come with insurance and gas.

As a subscriber, the customer gets the peace of mind of
knowing what their car expenses will be for years to come, as
well as a complete lack of hassle in buying, maintaining, and
trading a huge investment.

Better still, the subscription will be far cheaper than buying the car. Why? Because you've eliminated much of the car-
maker's risk. Because they know how many subscribers they
have and what their habits are, the carmakers won't have to
spend nearly as much on marketing, research, and product
risk. Instead they will be able to build a product for subscribers.

It's the milkman's revenge. Home delivery and inventory
management are coming back.

A Super-Low-Tech Way to Use Permission to Sell Cars

Joe Girard is listed in *Guinness* as the world's greatest car salesman. In a good year Joe sold ten times as many cars as the average car salesman, and he did it one car at a time.

How did Joe build such a career? He relied on Permission Marketing to build word of mouth.

If he's met you, he sends you twelve greeting cards a year. You'll hear from him on your birthday, his birthday, holidays, August 23, you name it. Of course, just about everyone is going to give you permission to send a birthday card!

Joe gets the attention of qualified prospects and existing customers for about twelve minutes a year. He uses that one minute each month to gently remind people that he is focused on them and is fun to do business with. He leverages this permission to turn strangers into friends. And, of course, the friends lead to new customers by word of mouth.

If someone knows someone who needs a car, he doesn't hesitate to recommend Joe. He knows his friend will enjoy the experience, and he knows that Joe is going to be around if something goes wrong.

This is simple, and it requires a few hours a day of Joe's time to coordinate, but it has tremendously altered Joe's career. Someday, when Joe retires and the cards stop, you can bet people will call. Probably thousands of people will notice. The anticipation in Joe's permission base is strong. The messages are relevant and personal. And they work.

WE'RE NOT IN THE AIRPLANE BUSINESS, WE'RE IN THE LOYALTY BUSINESS

American Airlines' AAdvantage program is one of the earliest and most successful examples of Permission Marketing. American gathers names and other pertinent information about their customers in the routine course of doing business. Since travel is frequently repeated, the customer grants permission, allowing American to gather more and more information about her as a customer. Each customer is tracked electronically and identified with a unique AAdvantage number.

American Airlines customers willingly accept, and often look forward to, updates on the award miles they've accumulated, along with special deals and bonus-mile destinations offered by American. AAdvantage customers "raise their hands" when they become AAdvantage members, and they "opt in" as they continue to fly American.

The main goal of American's frequent flier program is to increase customer loyalty through incentives and rewards. Frequent fliers receive special privileges, recognition, and mileage awards, so the more they fly, the more services and benefits they receive, and thus the more loyal they become. Loyalty is built upon customer satisfaction, and each successful transaction builds greater trust, one of the foundation blocks of Permission Marketing. With loyalty and trust (and a personal profile of each customer), American has the framework set up to take Permission Marketing to another level.

In addition to the American Airlines AAdvantage program mileage and activity summary, AAdvantage members receive a newsletter with travel-related bargains, offers, and of course new and improved services and benefits. But American Airlines also promotes non–American Airlines travel-related products. Through their monthly direct mailings, American AAdvantage customers learn about discounts and promotional offers by affiliate airlines. In addition, American offers discounts and special offers from rental car agencies, hotels, and wireless communication services, each clearly associated with the frequent traveler. And even though they're not in the travel industry, American teamed up with Citibank to offer the Citibank AAdvantage Visa or MasterCard, which allows customers to add miles to their account for each dollar they spend using the card.

With convenience and trust at the foundation of its customer base, American now offers AAdvantage customers non-travel-related products and services. They're leveraging the permission they have in ways that profit the member and American. American has developed affiliate promotions with securities brokers, even FTD retail florists (sending flowers when you're away from home may be a wise move).

If American screws up and doesn't send you your statement one month, odds are you'll miss it—and you might even call to complain. Imagine that. Complaining about not getting a piece of junk mail! They've created anticipation.

LEVERAGING A UTILITY'S RELATIONSHIP

While some phone company marketers are wasting the permission they've built around their phone bills (see page 192), others are realizing just how valuable permission can be.

Bell Atlantic recently sent me a letter that promises my family a $5 discount off my phone bill if we agree to receive special offers targeted to our interests by mail. All I have to do is fill out a simple six-question form and mail it in, postpaid. Bell Atlantic can now send me junk mail that is significantly more relevant and personal than traditional mail. And I'm more likely to read it.

By building an asset, they've taken a major step toward having an additional income stream. Even better, by applying a promotion on top of this program, they can go all the way and make the mailings *anticipated*. When they've done this, they'll discover that their response rates increase and the profitability of their permission base increases.

TURNING PERSONAL COMPUTER SOFTWARE INTO ONGOING SUBSCRIPTIONS

Sidekick is a personal organizer—software that manages your calendars, contacts, and communications. Starfish, the company that makes Sidekick, says their product "keeps you on time, on track, and in sync." Sidekick runs on your PC, of course, but it also runs on handheld products like the Palm Pilot and REX.

When you send in your registration card for Sidekick, you can arrange to have upgrade information and product offerings sent to you by e-mail. Almost everyone is interested in learning about product upgrades and add-on products that make your personal organization software more powerful and convenient. So customers raise their hands to receive offers on goodies that will make their lives more digitally organized. Then Starfish responds with an e-mail that fulfills the promise.

The e-mail gives the customer a chance to download free Sidekick companion products. You can get free Sidekick seasonal sports calendars and helpful home inventory cardfiles, for example, by clicking on the hot link right there in the e-mail. They offer Sidekick add-on products like instant HTML calendars and contact lists with a Sidekick Web Publisher (a tool for transforming Sidekick calendars and contact lists into Web pages).

When you buy a Palm Pilot, the registration card comes with another Permission Marketing offer. If you register your Palm Pilot with 3Com, they'll send you a free stylus (the little plastic pointer you use to point and click at things on the Palm Pilot screen). As part of the registration information, they ask for your e-mail address. So for the price of a plastic pen, most people raise their hand and offer 3Com their e-mail address. Using that e-mail address, 3Com informs Palm Pilot users about software upgrades.

Getting back to that first e-mail contact between Sidekick customers and Starfish (makers of Sidekick), Starfish also includes hot links to download their user manuals. So far, so good, since your permission brings you closer to a meaningful relationship based on value received. Then Starfish gives the already motivated user a chance to upgrade permission by offering her ever more opportunities. They include a link to the Starfish Daily Guide to the Oregon Shakespeare Festival, information on the Starfish coverage of the Iditarod Trail Sled Dog Race, and Starfish Software's Blazin' Chili recipe. In other words, they segue from what they know you're interested in and gently offer you the chance to upgrade your attention. But they are only links, so you don't have to go there if you're not curious.

A few weeks later the customer who has granted permission to receive e-mail from Starfish gets information about the availability of the latest version of Sidekick and a great offer that includes a game for your PC, free with your order. They also include information on how to synchronize data between Sidekick and other handheld devices like the Palm Pilot.

In other words, this is a Permission Marketing network. Any of the affiliate companies might be the one to get you to raise your hand and grant permission to exchange information, but they all intersect. Puma offers IntelliSync for Palm Pilot, and all the products can connect to Netcom. All these companies are part of one big permission circle. They are all relevant to you, the end user, because the products work together to provide solutions that can enhance your efficiency.

GOD IS A PERMISSION MARKETER

Bet you didn't know the Catholic charities were a marketer, did you? Forgive my tone, but understanding how even a cherished institution and benevolent charity uses these techniques makes the technique more clear for more ordinary businesses.

Every year they use Permission Marketing to raise lots of money for the church and local causes. They do this in just a few weeks, yet they never fail to reach their goal. How?

The church has overt permission to make a pitch to parishioners. People come to church expecting it, and the interaction between the priest and his flock is significant. It's the priest's job to sell parishioners on being charitable, so the messages he delivers aren't just expected, they're required. His parishioners expect him to deliver a message that is anticipated, relevant, and personal.

The priest leverages the permission earned by the church by marketing directly to his parishioners in a very straightforward, appropriate way. He speaks their language and understands their priorities. He customizes the message by making it relevant to each individual and by keeping his messages personal. And of course, each priest can personalize the appeal by asking only for an amount commensurate with their income.

Is it any wonder that they never miss a goal? They have God *and* permission on their side.

Record Clubs, the Grandfathers of Permission

Columbia Record Club is a classic Permission Marketer, focusing for years on this technique and measuring their results every step of the way.

As bait to get initial permission, Columbia offers consumers a passel of free albums. They leverage the permission into long-term record sales. They do this with a version of intravenous marketing called "negative option."

In negative option the marketer gets permission to send a notice of an upcoming delivery. If the consumer doesn't say "no," the marketer makes the shipment and bills the consumer. The negative option is at the core of their marketing strategy, and it has been incredibly profitable for them.

Moving forward, Columbia is using the Net as a tool for attracting and signing up new members. It also provides a cheaper way to implement the negative option.

However, the growth of their business is hindered by the mass market focus of selling hot albums to the core market of older teens. This demographic has ceased to grow very much and is very sensitive to hot and cold spells in the record business. Basically, if it's a year without a lot of great new records, Columbia suffers.

By enhancing their Permission Marketing techniques to increase relevance and personalization (their messages are already highly anticipated owing to the negative option), Columbia can make their business more profitable and reliable.

They could build a number of very profitable niches by identifying busy, affluent consumers who would cede decision making to Columbia if the bait was attractive enough. Thus, instead of having just four clubs (pop, classical, jazz, and country), they could have a hundred. Or a thousand.

Further, Columbia can also take advantage of the free frequency the Internet offers by having more impactful, frequent communications with members. This will increase personalization and lead to far greater loyalty.

Each of these clubs would increase the chances that consumers would allow Columbia to ship each month's selection. And by creating more of a subscription model, Columbia could offer heavy listeners two or three or ten a month, all with tremendous savings to the consumer.

The next steps are even more powerful. Once Columbia has a large base, a fast communication medium, and permission, it can start *commissioning* music based on the needs of its audience. If they know, for example, that a Lyle Lovett/ Willie Nelson duet has one hundred thousand advance orders, it's a lot easier to coax those two into the studio.

WHY YOU SEE AMERICAN EXPRESS APPLICATIONS AT SO MANY RESTAURANTS

American Express was an early king of Permission Marketing. In fact, American Express gets the consumer to *pay* Amex for permission! Even in the face of heavy competition, consumers pay $40, $100, or even $300 a year to carry an American Express card and to give American Express permission to market to them based on their behavior.

In exchange for this payment, American Express offers convenience and prestige to the user. Then the company devotes their considerable resources to leverage the permission they receive.

American Express sells information in aggregate on their card member base to merchants, who use the information to improve their marketing. For example, if you own a hotel, American Express might offer to tell you the top ten home zip codes of your competitors' best customers. What's that worth? By knowing where your competitors' customers are coming from, you can run ads in those markets. This technique would be impossible if American Express didn't have access to each card member's data.

Each Platinum card member receives a free glossy magazine every month, filled with beautiful photos and articles on exotic destinations. And of course, American Express sells advertising in those magazines.

The company uses the billing statements and other mailers to make special offers to their card members, upselling them to magazines, to stereos, and to other upscale items.

They have several divisions that create new products that would never sell unless they already had a permission relationship. One example of the power of their permission base is a video they acquired from a home improvement magazine. First they ran a computer check on the people who had purchased the video from the magazine. From that list, they computed what behavior and demographic patterns were likely to be found among buyers of the video. Then they used their database to find current American Express members that were most likely to have the same attributes as the original group of card members that bought the video.

The company then ran those patterns against their entire card member base and sent an ad for the video only to the most likely purchasers. Nearly 10 percent of them actually purchased the video—about seven times what you might expect. Because the ad was relevant, it did better. It would have done better still if it had been personal and expected, of course.

Another example is their annual hardcover desk calendar, which is a multimillion-dollar continuity program. They offer card members the first year's book for free, in exchange for permission to send it again every year (intravenous level permission).

Consumers sign up because the bait is compelling (free book) and because they trust American Express. Year after year the book is anticipated (after all, you need something to write in every year) and relevant (you signed up for it). The end result is very low risk and very high profit for American Express.

The shame of the Amex story is that when faced with competition from cheaper cards with better benefits, American Express hasn't countered with more sophisticated Permission Marketing techniques. Instead they have been chewing away at the permission they were already granted.

Now, the offers they make aren't as personal or relevant. The quality of their prestige is decreasing, making the communications far less privileged and effective. Each brand manager with American Express can profit by selling one more item using their permission asset. But over time the entire organization suffers as the asset they've carefully nurtured is traded for short-term profits.

Some People Eat a Pint of Ice Cream Every Night

Here's how a superpremium ice cream used Permission Marketing to maintain market share and build profitability.

It turns out that only 600,000 to 800,000 people account for the core users of this very rich, very expensive ice cream. These are folks who are really serious about sitting down on the couch with a pint of superrich mocha fudge. In fact, there are a substantial number of these people who buy one hundred pints a year.

The problem, of course, is that reaching them and keeping them from switching brands is very expensive. Every time the company runs an interruption ad on TV or in a magazine, they're reaching one hundred casual users for every serious one. Worse, the incentives they offer the casual users might cost them more than they help the brand.

This ice-cream company, working with a top direct marketer, decided to build a permission base of heavy users. Scraping together names from previous promotions and other interactions they'd had, they created a mailing to probable prospects.

The results were fairly extraordinary—24 percent of the recipients enrolled in an ice-cream club! A response rate of 24 percent in print direct mail is essentially unheard of, but because the marketer was offering a chance to have a dialogue, they hit the right nerve. Users filled out a survey, giving details about habits, kids, and their favorite flavors. And they agreed to receive regular updates from the brand about recipes, new products, and more.

The bait was a chance to keep in touch with what was obviously an important brand for them. And the coupons that came along with every interaction didn't hurt, either.

Today there are more than 100,000 people (almost 15 percent of all the core users) in this club, and the frequent interactions, the recipes, the caring, and the growing permission levels are all leading to the creation of a marketing fortress that will prevent competitors from scooping this company moving forward.

SOME MAGAZINES DON'T NEED NEWSSTANDS

Can a magazine use permission to increase its effectiveness?

Remedy magazine is aimed at the growing market of

consumers age fifty or over, with a special focus on health and wellness. Rather than launching it as a traditional magazine, however, it was created as a Permission Marketing vehicle.

You can't subscribe to *Remedy* for any price. It's free. In exchange, all 2.2 million subscribers have filled out a comprehensive two-page survey about their health, including details about prescription drugs, savings accounts, even mouthwash usage and eyedrops.

Remedy scrupulously observes the rules of permission. They don't rent or sell the data to anyone. But they do use the data to make the magazine more relevant and to include advertising that is personal to the consumer.

An amazing 35 percent of the people who receive one free sample copy of *Remedy* by mail fill out this survey in order to keep the issues coming. They've given *Remedy* permission to market to them, and they respond by paying attention.

The best part is the renewal rate. After two years of getting the magazine, people trust *Remedy* to keep its end of the bargain. They know that the company has respected the permission, and they respond by giving even more data. When faced with a daunting, personal four-page survey, an astonishing 73 percent of the subscribers renew by sending it back completed.

The question facing an advertiser is a simple one: Given a choice between running a random interruption ad in a magazine that goes to everyone or running a targeted ad to this core group of people who have given permission, which is likely to be more effective?

PERMISSION EVEN WORKS FOR A CHEMICAL ENGINEER WORKING AS A HOUSEPAINTER

Permission Marketing techniques don't always require fancy databases and significant investments. They even work for a small-business entrepreneur like Zygi Szpak.

Zygi is a Polish émigré who is a master of painting and drywall. He's created a significant income by using Permission Marketing to turn small jobs into big jobs and to create word of mouth that leads to ever more work.

He begins by meeting someone through word of mouth—his reputation leads to referrals. After a brief meeting, Zygi gets permission to do a small job—usually painting a room—for an unbelievably low cost. Because Zygi does the work himself, he can still turn a profit, and he's sure to do an exceptional job.

Zygi overdelivers on his promise, thus creating trust and goodwill. He leverages the permission he has earned to go on a tour of the house with the owner, together identifying projects the homeowner would like to tackle next.

Based on his past overdelivery, he earns the right to take on other projects in the house, each bigger than the first, each more profitable as well. Having overcome the fear that goes with hiring a new contractor, he becomes the safe choice and can thus build more profit into each ensuing job.

Over time he leverages his first job into four or five or ten projects, each more elaborate and profitable than the last. However, he always offers high value and quality.

I know this works, because Zygi has done more than a dozen jobs for me, and after we introduced him to our new neighborhood, he found no fewer than ten new clients, each of whom followed the same pattern. And it must be working, because Zygi's driving a shiny new van around the neighborhood.

Compare this approach with that of the typical contractor, who attempts to earn the maximum amount on each job yet spends most of his time looking for new work and earning nothing during his downtime. Without a loyal base, the word of mouth isn't as forthcoming, further compounding the typical contractor's woes.

SELLING CRIBS TO HOSPITALS

Permission Marketing works in a business-to-business setting as well.

Hard Manufacturing is the number-one manufacturer of hospital cribs in the world. These stainless-steel-and-chrome cribs are virtually indestructible, and the price tag and profit margins reflect their durability and specialized nature.

With more than three-quarters of the market, the challenges facing Hard are how to grow the market and how to be sure that customers are buying the best crib they can afford by upgrading them whenever possible (more advanced models cost more).

After several years of using traditional techniques to interrupt the purchasing agents at hospitals (magazines, mailings, and trade shows), and after spending thousands of dollars mailing unsolicited catalogs to possible prospects, Hard decided to adopt a permission approach.

The first insight was that they sell almost all of their

products to the chief pediatric nurse at major hospitals. While the orders may come from the purchasing department, this nurse is almost always the key player.

Hard bought a mailing list of this audience and interrupted them with a mailing asking them to fill out a survey about what they really want in future cribs. The bait—the selfish benefit for the nurse—is the chance to give an opinion.

Over time, a huge percentage of the pediatric nurses targeted has given permission. Sometimes Hard offers these nurses a chance to enter a drawing for a free TV, sometimes it's just a cheerful card, but by using frequent messages, they've been able to begin "dating" each of these nurses.

Hard leverages the permission by sending engineers into the field to actually design new cribs with feedback from these key decision makers. If the marketing messages didn't feel personal and relevant before these trips, they most definitely do now. The nurses are delighted when they are credited with developing innovations in new crib models—some of which even carry the names of the hospitals with which they were designed.

When each new crib is complete, Hard has complete and total permission to market to these key players with a high level of attention on their part. The asset they've built is at least as valuable as their factory—it's easy to buy a factory, but much more challenging to assemble a loyal and accessible base of decision makers.

Internet Case Studies

AOL Wants to Be Your Buying Agent

Bob Pittman and Steve Case at America Online have a vision of how permission will totally transform their company and the way goods are sold.

As the company has grown, they've explored a number of marketing techniques, some good and some bad.

The good news is that they recognized early on that they can use permission to dramatically increase the user base of the service. Jan Brandt is the brilliant marketer behind the dozens of AOL disks you have in your house. As mentioned earlier, at their peak AOL was spending an astonishing $300 in marketing to attract each new member to the service.

Obviously they had no chance of extracting $300 in connect fees from users, given that the average life span of a user is less than a year and it costs only $20 a month (of which most goes to pay for phone lines and the like).

So why bother spending that sort of money? Jan realized that the best way to get a long-term customer was to do whatever it takes to get a trial customer. A free trial is a very effective tool for teaching people what AOL could do. And once that free trial is under way, many of those who gave the first level of permission continue with the service and upgrade that permission. The second level includes

- permission to store their charge card.
- permission to handle their e-mail.

- permission to put notices and ads in front of them in a nonintrusive way.

This permission is astonishingly powerful. Using it (though some would say abusing it), they've leveraged the permission to promote TeleSave, a remarketer of low-cost residential phone service.

After putting $100 million up front to get AOL's attention, TeleSave has signed up more than 400,000 AOL customers to its phone service. The cost of sign-up is very low because they use the free frequency and high interruption power of AOL to get people's attention and then leverage trust with AOL to make a no-name brand palatable.

Next they use the power of the medium and the fact that AOL already has a credit card on file to make billing simple and cheap. And because the billing is so fast and easy, the permission granted to TeleSave is greater than that most people give AT&T or MCI.

Who's really adding value here—TeleSave or AOL? AOL holds all the cards. Because it is AOL that holds the permission, AOL can pick and choose among long-distance providers in search of the best deal. And if they're smart and focused on the long run, AOL will search for the best deal for AOL *and* for their consumers.

Along the way, AOL has burned some of their very expensive, hard-earned permission. In a rush to maximize long-distance sign-ups, they've relied on a very dangerous tactic. Instead of rewarding the consumer in an ongoing way, they punish their users with a pop-up screen.

A pop-up screen is a page that shows up on AOL as the

user is moving through the service. The only way to get past the screen and get to where you were headed is to click the Order or the Cancel button.

These full-page screens interrupt the AOL session completely. They cannot be ignored, and they won't go away until the consumer chooses to accept whatever is being offered or declines. Worse, they're often aimed at everyone, so they're usually irrelevant.

By using invasive screens that interrupt the user experience to hawk an item that's often completely inappropriate to the user, they create a high level of churn and high costs for AOL.

AOL is now becoming aware of the high cost of annoying users so casually, and I expect they will soon find more gentle, permission-based ways to get attention and grow permission.

Over time, look for AOL to integrate its incredibly powerful asset to become a major provider of life insurance, financial services, real estate, and other products with high profit margins taking the place of high cost of sales.

As AOL gets more and more permission from consumers, the $20 monthly fee will be dwarfed by hundreds or thousands of dollars a month in expenses that users are paying to subscribe to a wide variety of products and services. AOL becomes a permission channel!

As AOL gets more permission (provided they don't abuse members with innovations like pop-up screens), they will be able to provide ever more messages that are anticipated, relevant, and personal. By dramatically cutting the costs of marketing and billing, AOL can reinvent a significant slice of our world.

At its ultimate, it's not hard to image AOL collecting $1,000 to $10,000 to $30,000 per year, *per customer*. After all, if they've helped you find a mortgage, buy a house, choose a cellular provider, and even subscribe to a car, a huge amount of money flows through their doors—all because they acquired permission and moved people up the permission ladder.

BonusMail from Intellipost

BonusMail is a free service that connects advertisers with consumers via e-mail. The consumers "raise their hands" by filling out a customer profile to get promotional information about subjects they're interested in. They can choose from the following list of subjects:

Books & Literature
Business News
Computers/Communication
Events & Nightlife
Financial Services & Investments
Health & Fitness
Home Hobbies
Music & Entertainment
Science & Technology
Sports—Spectator
Sports—Active
Travel

The incentive to receive these targeted "e-mail ads" comes in the form of gift points called Rew@rds credits. With each e-mail message they receive, they also receive credits good for free frequent flier miles, gift certificates, meals, and other things. Every time a customer gets another BonusMail message, Intellipost automatically posts credits to the customer's account.

If the consumer replies to the e-mail, thus giving Intellipost notice that she's not only received the e-mail but read it, too, Intellipost tacks on even more Rew@rds credits. Some advertisers even offer bonus credits for responding to their offers. And each time a consumer receives a message, her Rew@rds balance is included in the e-mail. That way the consumer can easily keep track of her balance and redeem the Rew@rds credits for prizes whenever she wants.

The Permission Marketing at work here is limited by the consumer and protected by safeguards provided by Intellipost. With these in place, the consumer experiences a level of security that encourages him to continue granting permission. One of the important features of BonusMail, for example, is that the consumer receives only offers associated with things that interest him. In addition, the consumer gets to choose how often he wants to receive these "e-mail ads," selecting from several options: every other day, once a day, twice a day, three times a day, or an unlimited number of e-mail ads per day. And each consumer also has the option to halt the BonusMail offers and communications at any time.

Then there is the anonymity factor, which is supplied by Intellipost for the protection of each consumer. Intellipost does not sell or exchange any personal information (name, e-mail address, or mailing address) to anyone. They don't release personal information to any other party without the consumer's express permission. When they do give information to advertisers, it is in the form of grouped statistics compiled from all participating members' answers to survey questions. And the BonusMail system was designed to make it impossible for advertisers to extract any personal information on their own.

Basically, BonusMail is paying people for attention. Not that there's anything wrong with that. By making the deal overt and measurable, they've taken direct mail to a new level.

CyberGold

CyberGold, like Intellipost's BonusMail, matches advertisers with consumers via e-mail. The advertisers pay each time a consumer reads an ad, but rather than receive gift certificates or merchandise, the consumer receives cash. Customers may be asked to visit a Web site, or the advertiser may pitch the consumer about a product. Either way, the advertiser pays the consumers for their attention. CyberGold makes money by charging advertisers a commission each time a customer reads one of their ads.

To "raise their hands," consumers provide their e-mail address, the country in which they reside (CyberGold is currently available only in the United States and Canada), and a password to prevent someone else from accidentally (or intentionally) ordering products or making transactions on behalf of the consumer. Once the consumer provides these three things, he is eligible to receive special offers and start earning CyberGold credits.

To convert CyberGold into cash, the consumer needs to provide more detailed personal information. The consumer may choose to release this personal information to the companies of her choice, and for billing and shipping purposes, but CyberGold does not divulge this information without the consumer's permission.

As for what goes on behind the scenes at CyberGold, here's how it works. Advertisers set up a debit account that remains inactive until a consumer interacts with their ad—plays a game, purchases a product, or checks out a Web site. Upon completing an advertiser's request, the consumer is paid in CyberGold, which are credits that accrue in the consumer's account. CyberGold then charges a small fee to the advertiser for connecting them with the consumer and facilitating the transaction. The consumer is guaranteed cash for paying attention, and the advertisers are guaranteed that the consumer saw the ad.

There are several types of offers and rewards based on various types of participation:

Attention Tests: These are offers that require only a few moments of Web surfing and maybe answering a few quick questions.

Purchase Rewards: These offers pay the consumer when he buys a product. These usually require a credit card.

Pending Rewards: These are usually rewards given for purchasing or signing up. However, CyberGold credits aren't rewarded immediately. Sometimes the business wants to verify an order first, in which case CyberGold is credited to the consumer's account after the processing is complete (usually just a few days).

As with all successful Permission Marketing efforts, CyberGold keeps customer information strictly confidential. To help guarantee privacy, CyberGold uses a company called TRUSTe, an independent, nonprofit, privacy initiative dedicated to building users' trust and confidence on the Internet (mentioned earlier in the book).

Value America

Value America is an Internet retail store that sells a wide array of consumer goods, everything from shower faucets to wide-screen TVs. They claim to be able to sell for less, since they deal with so many manufacturers and in such large quantities. They also provide certain conveniences that are possible only through the power of the Internet. But what Value America offers that really sets them apart is a series of value-added enticements as they roll out their Permission Marketing strategy.

As part of the Permission Marketing game plan, the Value America home page tells you that you don't have to be a member to get product information. You don't have to be a member to buy things, either. But members not only get an optimized product presentation, they generally get a better price on the products offered by Value America. Members get other goodies, too, like a product "supply and accessory" link. Anyone who has tried to find a replacement toner cartridge for a laser printer, or keep the decor of a room consistent, or find an ink cartridge for a particular pen, knows how difficult it can be to find items or accessories that go with a specific item.

Members can view a list of products they have purchased at Value America, along with a link to lists of all products and accessories that are related to that particular item. So instead of having to figure out the model number of your printer, and then figure out which of the numerous and similar ink cartridges fit it, the matching is already done for you. Click on the picture of your printer, select the cartridge that appears, and Value America delivers it.

Obviously, the more you buy from them, the easier it is. The list of purchased products gets longer, it's easier to find matching products, and ValueAmerica can offer you discounts.

The only information they require for membership is your name and a password. However, by completing the entire member profile, you raise your hand further by giving permission to record your purchases. If you give them your address, they automatically fill in the ship to and billing addresses when you purchase a product. With answers to certain demographic questions, they can better understand the kinds of shoppers they're dealing with, thus helping them to make better decisions as to what products to carry and which manufacturers to support, which means better prices for their customers. By becoming a member, you can even select your favorite charity, which Value America donates to in your name based on the amount of your purchases.

Raising your hand and granting Value America permission to know you better has other benefits, too, like Value America Dollars, which lower the cost of your next purchase. As a member you are eligible for this program, which puts at least 1 percent of your purchase amount (sometimes more) in a special account that you can spend on future Value America purchases. But if you don't tell them who you are, they can't keep track of your purchases, so this benefit is strictly for members.

With Value America you get the convenience of shopping

at a store that knows you, remembers what you've bought, and even adjusts the scope of its presentations to meet the capabilities of your computer. So what else can they offer? How about an automated calendar system to automatically remind you about certain upcoming dates that are associated with buying someone a present?

Value America has made some broad promises, and they've obviously got work to do before they can deliver on all of them. But by building a business around the power of permission, it's likely that they have a significant head start over their more traditional competition.

Amazon.com

Most traditional book publishers make a huge percentage of their new sales by distributing best-sellers through the major retail book chains like Barnes & Noble and Borders. One Tom Clancy makes up for a whole bunch of unread poetry collections.

Amazon.com started shaking things up a few years ago with an entirely new business model housed within their Web site. Instead of aiming at people who go to bookstores and buy best-sellers, their marketing model focuses on consumer needs and selling primarily midlist or backlist books, which they feature on their Web site. The Amazon top ten has little or nothing in common with *The New York Times Book Review* Best Seller List.

They couple this approach with their own flavor of Permission Marketing, which doesn't start until you buy your first book. (Amazon.com doesn't ask for anything from you, not even your name, until you make a purchase.)

Once you raise your hand to become an Amazon.com customer, they begin collecting information about you. If you're a member of a specialized interest group (art, cooking, travel), you probably tend to buy more than one book on that particular subject. But considering how difficult it can be to find what's out there, Amazon.com uses the information they collect about you to make an educated guess about what you'd like to read. Then they make book selections and gently guide you toward them. The service provided by Amazon.com makes it unnecessary to trudge around town to bookstores, looking for books on a particular subject they know you're already interested in. Amazon.com does the legwork for you.

Amazon does this in a subtle way. Instead of sending you a regular e-mail with their top picks, they focus on creating communities and providing relevant links throughout their site.

Amazon.com doesn't ask you for a lot of personal information because they have no way to use it (yet). They do ask for your e-mail address. But even your name is optional until you buy a book. Then they assign you a unique customer ID that allows them to track your Web site travels while visiting Amazon.com, and thus they could, in theory, see which books might interest you and where your interests lie.

Amazon.com's strategy still looks a lot like mass marketing, but it portends a powerful one-to-one marketing future. Today, if you've ever bought a book from them and you go to their Web site, a message will appear at the top of the screen that reads "Personal Recommendations"—which is a real-time lookup of other clients' most recent purchases. It's not highly researched and not guaranteed to be of interest to the

Web site visitor, but there are some selection criteria in place. David Risher, Amazon.com's senior VP of product development, says, "We're about one percent of the way there," in terms of targeting specific customers with tailored book offerings. They clearly see the implications and the opportunity.

Amazon.com is in the process of integrating a software solution called BookMatcher. It will work only to the degree that customer permission includes complete and accurate answers to questions about their interests. With that information it will start recommending selections, augmenting your customer profile with what it learns from each of your ensuing queries and purchases. But for now, 98 percent of their e-mail customer contact is done in aggregate—much like bulk e-mail. If you are a science-fiction buff, for example, you're on the science-fiction book e-mail update list.

So while their one-to-one marketing efforts are less than totally one-to-one, they are using their permission-based asset to expand their product breadth. In addition to books, Amazon.com offers videos and CDs to customers and is in the process of developing their marketing approach to compete with online merchants like CDnow and Music Boulevard. Eventually they will have an even greater opportunity to capitalize on their growing permission-based audience.

InfoBeat

"Surf, search, and sift no more—InfoBeat will deliver personalized news straight to your e-mail box." That's the introduction to InfoBeat on the home page of their colorful Web site, which offers customers a free, customizable Web filter. InfoBeat gathers current news on topics you select and delivers it to your e-mail address at the times you've requested. You choose from front-page headlines, TV listings, horoscopes, sports scores, specific stock quotes, weather, and more.

The cost of this service is your permission to receive text and multimedia ads imbedded in your customized messages. As a customer, you fill out an application. They ask for your name, e-mail address, gender, birthday, zip code, marital status, computer used, number of children in your home, your education, employment status, occupation, company size, and if you own your own home. Ads are targeted and personalized.

So far, they've got more than 3 million subscribers, making them bigger than all but a dozen magazines in the print world.

My Yahoo!

If you've been on the Internet, you've heard of Yahoo!. Yahoo! offers a multitude of things beyond the famous Yahoo! search engine. In fact, the Yahoo! home page has about fifty hot links to all kinds of stuff, including entertainment, weather, and stock quotes. I even saw a contest to win a trip to a Willie Nelson picnic. Anyway, one of the links gets you to a subset of Yahoo! called My Yahoo!, a site that offers special options if you are willing to volunteer some personal information.

The information they ask is pretty simple and not that personal. They want your birthday in case you forget your password (that's how they verify it's you). They ask what industry you're in, your occupation, and your zip code. There's an optional section that asks you to choose from a list of in-

terests, like sports, music, and shopping, which they say enables them to choose the kind of news, Web sites, and information they should display on your individual pages. (Just
prior to asking that, however, they mention that from time to
time they'd like to contact you about "specials and new products.") Naturally (but graciously) they also ask for your
e-mail address, right next to a radio button you can click on
that reads "Please don't contact me."

That's the information you give up. What you get in return from My Yahoo! is a user ID and password that lets you
do lots of things nonregistered users can't do. Registered
users can customize the look of My Yahoo! to their own personal tastes. In fact, My Yahoo! has a succinct and alluring
solicitation—"It's yours. You build it. It's free." Indeed, you
get to pick only what you want to see. You personalize your
Internet experience. That means you can tailor each Yahoo!
page so it displays what you want. This may sound trivial, but
there's an incredible amount of value in letting My Yahoo! do
all your filtering with a single mouse click.

On the front page you can set up the section called "Headlines" to reflect just the news you want to read. From the
"Business and Technology" section you might be interested in
reading only about biotechnology, medical, and pharmaceuti-
cals, and perhaps MSNBC Business News. As for sports, say
you're not interested in anything but tennis and rugby. Select
those options, and you won't read a word about the Dodgers
or the Celtics.

Then there's your personal information sections (non-
headline news). Say you trade stocks and want your "Personal Finance" section to reflect quotes, your portfolio, and

recent upgrades and downgrades. Then on the other side of your screen you want a currency converter and a Web site tracker. Make those menu selections, and seconds later you're looking at the data screen of your choice. You choose what to include or exclude, and you can customize as often as you'd like. Customize the "Business" section, "Health" section, "Entertainment" section, "Travel" section, and others. And once you have it all set up the way you want it, will you use it? Of course! And what did it cost you? Permission to exchange information about yourself and to set up a communication channel to receive information about things that interest you.

Yahoo! can now deliver you content that is anticipated, relevant, and personal. They don't yet have an active way to establish an e-mail connection with you that makes it complete. You have to remember to go back and look at the stuff. But there's no question that the right ad in the right spot in this medium will be far more effective than an ordinary banner somewhere else.

Yoyodyne

Yoyodyne has built an online system optimized for Permission Marketing. The programs we create follow a simple three-part process:

1. Attract targeted consumers with banner ads promising a great prize. Interested consumers get more information by clicking on the banner, which takes them to a registration page.
2. Inform consumers about the promotion and have them enter their e-mail address on a registration Web page.

3. Engage the consumer in a high-frequency Web and e-mail correspondence in which participation is rewarded with ever
greater chances to win the prize.

By appealing to one of the simplest human desires (the
joy of winning) and balancing it with judicious doses of relevant information, we capture and keep attention.

For H&R Block, for example, Yoyodyne was assigned to
build interest and knowledge of their new Premium Tax service. This was a challenge for three reasons. First, no one on
earth had ever heard of this service. Second, learning about a
new tax service isn't high on anyone's list of ways to spend a
Saturday. And third, the upper-income group targeted by the
service was unlikely to think of H&R Block when it came
time to do their taxes.

The ordinary strategy for Block would be to buy magazine advertising—in *Time* or *U.S. News & World Report*.
However, the client and their agency (WCJ Chicago) both
knew that with the budget available, they'd never be able to
interrupt enough people to cut through the clutter.

Instead we used the Net. The banners were simple. They
read, "Play the H&R Block We'll Pay Your Taxes Game."

About 60,000 people clicked on the banner. After clicking,
they saw a registration page that explained that in order to
have their taxes paid next year (up to $25,000), they had to
answer a bunch of trivia questions about Block and taxes over
the next ten weeks.

More than 50,000 people eagerly enrolled. Now, with
their permission and their e-mail address, we went to work.
Twice a week for ten weeks we sent these 50,000 people an

e-mail about the game and about Premium Tax. We drove people to Block's Web site to look up answers to tax trivia questions and created a curriculum that taught people about the benefits of H&R Block and Premium Tax.

Each e-mail averaged a 36 percent response rate. This is an astonishingly high response rate for a direct response campaign—the average in direct mail is closer to 2 percent.

H&R Block saw a noticeable improvement in traffic to their site and, more important, saw traffic to all parts of their site. Because every e-mail we sent was different for each person, the notes were personal. They were opened because they contained a score—valuable information that made the message me-mail instead of e-mail.

But the real results were unveiled in a postgame survey. We sent a multiple-choice question about Premium Tax to three different groups:

- People on the Net who didn't enroll.
- People in the promotion who enrolled but didn't respond even once.
- People in the promotion who were regular responders.

For people who didn't enroll, random chance would have led to about 20 percent of the surveys being returned correctly. Among people on the Net in general, only 18 percent of the respondents got the right answer. Essentially, among the general public, there was no knowledge at all of what the service offered.

Among enrollees who didn't play, 34 percent got the question right. This means that even though people weren't participating actively, they were reading the mail! It means that a statistically relevant amount of learning went on, even among passive participants.

Finally, among people who were active players, an incredible 54 percent knew the right answer.

The power of permission played a big role. Because the messages were anticipated, personal, and relevant, people paid attention. And because there was a curriculum, they learned.

In a very different promotion, Yoyodyne is working to motivate online consumers to start shopping.

We believe e-commerce is a huge potential growth area for the Net, and many people believe that it will become the driving economic force behind the Web.

But for every Amazon.com there are dozens of merchants who have just a few customers online. And for every consumer who does all his gift shopping online, there are hundreds who aren't willing to buy anything.

EZSpree was designed to put promotion into shopping online. Consumers are so used to promotions in the offline world (big sale!, clearance!, buy one get one free!) that they've come to expect that from any shopping experience. Yet just before Christmas 1997, the world of online merchants was sterile, confusing, and not very appealing.

EZSpree offered consumers two very important benefits. First, one lucky consumer would win a $100,000 shopping spree. Second, all the stores in the EZSpree promotion were researched and approved, vastly improving the sense of security for consumers who had never shopped online.

In order to opt in and give permission, a consumer saw

one of our banners and came to the EZSpree site. He gave us his e-mail address and read the rules of the game.

In order to be eligible to win, a consumer had to visit ten different store windows. Each store (more than 250 were featured) had the opportunity to choose four items and post them in their window. So instead of offering consumers a confusing array of thousands of choices, merchants were forced to pick just four items that represented their store.

In a study audited by KPMG, we discovered that the click-through rates on the store windows to the store itself ranged from 10 percent to an astonishing 44 percent. The average was more than 18 percent. To put this into perspective, the click-through rate on banners averages less than 1 percent.

This demonstrates that when they see a compelling and relevant offer, consumers will often raise their hands and opt in. By driving consumers to six different store windows and sending nearly 20 percent of those visits into the stores themselves, Yoyodyne created an environment where consumers were very likely to do what we asked.

Fourteen percent of the consumers enrolled in the promotion actually bought something. And many of them were shopping online for the first time ever.

The back end of the promotion is just as important. Every week consumers received an e-mail. It featured special offers and was tailored for each consumer. If you visited lots of men's clothing stores, we could send you a note with a special offer about another men's clothing store.

Even better, the mail included your "score," how many more store windows you needed to visit to be eligible for the grand prize.

What is a permission base of motivated shoppers worth? If an online merchant makes money from every incremental sale, how profitable is it to be able to contact, with fully customized, relevant, personal notes, consumers who are interested in your store?

The power of anticipated direct mail with free stamps can't be overstated. Busy consumers are eager and willing to participate in this sort of dialogue—as long as the marketer follows the basic rules of permission.

ELEVEN

How to Evaluate a Permission Marketing Program

If you measure it, it will get done.

THERE ARE TEN QUESTIONS TO ASK when evaluating any marketing program:

1. What's the bait?
2. What does an incremental permission cost?
3. How deep is the permission that is granted?
4. How much does incremental frequency cost?
5. What's the active response rate to communications?
6. What are the issues regarding compression?
7. Is the company treating the permission as an asset?
8. How is the permission being leveraged?
9. How is the permission level being increased?
10. What is the expected lifetime of one permission?

Here's a more in-depth look at each question.

1. What's the Bait?

What will the selfish consumer respond to? Is there a clear and obvious benefit being offered to each consumer, or is there a contest or promotion that offers an even better benefit to a select group of consumers?

There's no room for subtlety or selfish behavior on the part of the marketer here. Marketers that offer better bait with a more obvious benefit will always attract more consumers than their competition.

The best bait is easy to describe, coveted by a large portion of your target market and economical to deliver. And the bait must be tangible enough that the consumer will give up precious attention and privacy to participate.

Choosing the right bait is essential. It must also resonate with the product or service you offer. If there's a high overlap between the bait and the ultimate message, you're far more likely to attract and keep the right people.

For example, when Yoyodyne ran a promotion for AT&T aimed at college students, the bait was a trip for five to a beach house for spring break. This was ideal for a few reasons:

• It attracted just college students.
• It played up the idea of community and friends, which has a high overlap with phone service.
• It wasn't expensive, yet it was "life changing" for the winner because few college students have the money or initiative to put it together themselves.
• It was vivid and easy to describe.

Obviously bait doesn't have to be a prize. It could be a coupon, information about an interesting subject, entertainment, or membership to a privileged group.

2. What Does an Incremental Permission Cost?

How much does it cost to get one more person to sign up to participate? Offline, this is computed by dividing the cost of ads by the number of expected participants. In direct mail and online, it's a straightforward analysis of media costs divided by permission.

Permission always costs something. Tracking it and figuring out its worth is essential if you want to maximize the return on your investment.

3. How Deep Is the Permission That Is Granted?

This is a critical metric. If someone gives you the right to send him a catalog, that's all he's given you. Being overt about exactly what the consumer can expect ensures that there will be no misunderstandings and no canceled permissions.

4. How Much Does Incremental Frequency Cost?

How much does it cost to send one more marketing message to one more person? In direct mail this number could be thirty cents up to a dollar or two if you're sending catalogs. Online, the number is zero.

Choosing the right frequency mechanism and the right media for your audience maximizes your yield.

5. What's the Active Response Rate to Communications?

After you've gained permission and begun to send out messages, how many people write back? How many take action based on the messages? How can you use a feedback loop to increase the personalization and the relevance of the messages over time?

With testing, you can undoubtedly increase this number, often by two or five times.

6. What Are the Issues Regarding Compression?

Do you have a feedback loop and technology in place to increase the bait as its effectiveness begins to tail off? For example, American Airlines could monitor fliers and discover when their travel habits started to taper off—perhaps indicating that they were switching to another airline. This would be a great opportunity to follow up with some additional rewards to recapture the interest and enthusiasm of this consumer.

If it costs a company $100 to attract a new customer but only $5 in additional anticompression rewards to keep her, the choice is pretty obvious.

7. Is the Company Treating the Permission as an Asset?

Companies measure their assets every day. The inventory in the factory or the amount of money in the bank is closely watched. Are you measuring your permission base? Each marketer in the organization should be acutely aware of exactly how wide and how deep this permission is.

Over time, this asset can be leveraged and increased. Both take an investment, but as with all assets, if that investment is measured over time, the ROI can be computed.

8. How Is the Permission Being Leveraged?

Once a permission base is built, it is possible to leverage it. When you have permission to talk with relevance and personalization to a large number of people, you can piggyback new messages to the group and dramatically increase profits.

For example, introducing Orvis clothing to loyal purchasers of Orvis fishing gear is a smart use of the company's number one asset—their right to talk to well-heeled fishing buffs.

In addition to leveraging new product sales, marketers can try to increase consumption of existing products or partner with other companies to gradually share permission.

American Airlines does this with hotels, for example. Instead of renting the names of its frequent fliers to a hotel chain, it features the hotels in the anticipated monthly mailing to its loyal customer base. If some of those consumers end up at the hotel, American has successfully leveraged their ability to talk with these individuals.

9. How Is the Permission Level Being Increased?

Once the permission pattern is set, the obligation of the marketer is to increase it. Without proper care, the permission will fade. But by focusing on how to earn more and more trust from the prospect, the marketer can increase the permission, making it a more valuable asset over time.

Amazon.com is in the midst of this process. At the beginning of the relationship, the permission is slim indeed. A consumer is happy to be reminded periodically of something of interest at Amazon but isn't anticipating e-mail from the company.

By running a promotion with modest but fun prizes, Amazon is able to get much more active participation from a portion of its list. It moves consumers up the permission ladder and makes its mailings anticipated.

The next step would be to get more personal and relevant. Once Amazon knows the kinds of books you like, it can sign you up for an automatic review service. Or a special discount program on a book chosen every month based on your interest.

The next level is to sign people up for book clubs and get their permission to select a book and send it on approval in exchange for a discount or some other benefit.

10. What Is the Expected Lifetime of One Permission?

The final question goes to the lifetime value of the permission. If permission is transient—as it is, say, at a tourist attraction—then the amount the marketer is willing to invest should be less than it would be when the permission can last a very long time.

Marketers win when they can convert what many perceive to be a short-term permission cycle to one that lasts for a much longer period of time. Grocery stores, for example, are working with Catalina Marketing to turn the one-shot nature of the supermarket experience into a loyalty program that can last for months or even years.

By spreading the cost of acquiring a new customer over a longer period of time, a grocery store can dramatically outpace its competition.

TWELVE

The Permission FAQ

The most frequently asked questions about Permission Marketing

1. Do You Need a Web Site to Do This?

No. Permission Marketing works in any medium where the consumer can be engaged in a dialogue. It works in an airport terminal, by direct mail, on the telephone, and online. And marketing campaigns in any medium can be equipped with a Permission Marketing component as well.

For example, every TV commercial ought to have an 800 number or e-mail address where people who want to "raise their hands" can go for more information. This starts the dialogue going.

Walking through the Cincinnati airport last week, I participated in a great example of Permission Marketing run by Skytel.

Skytel's challenge is to get its beepers into the hands of people like me. Folks who might need one but have never been persuaded that it's worth the hassle and the money.

Rather than running an expensive ad campaign that had no chance to get my attention, never mind my business, Skytel rented a booth at the airport. By staffing it with an outgoing, engaging human being, they cut through the clutter and got my attention.

I had a few minutes between flights, I was there, and the offer was compelling—get a free beeper for a month. So I gave the sales rep permission to talk with me for a minute.

She used situational permission to give me a one-minute sales pitch. The offer was straightforward and relevant. I could get a beeper for a month, no strings attached. If I didn't like it, I could place it in the envelope (which was prepaid!) and ship it back.

The beeper was already set up, the instructions were simple, and I had nothing to lose. I moved up to the next level of permission.

I now have the free beeper. The sales rep has sent me a follow-up letter (which I read, because I know her), and she's also followed up with a phone call to see if it's working okay.

This is classic Permission Marketing. Over time, if Skytel is as smart as I think they are, they'll refine and target the messages they send to me to make them even more personal and relevant. And if my behavior begins to lag, I expect they'll invest in promotions that will make my interactions with them personally profitable as well.

Can Skytel use this permission to make even more money? Of course. They can start selling me cellular phones, on-the-road workstations, an entire range of services that matches the permission I've already given them.

2. Does Permission Marketing Work Only with Consumers?

Actually, the business-to-business opportunities for this technique are at least as compelling as the offerings for consumers.

The real challenge in business-to-business marketing is the huge cost of contacting prospects. Unlike mass marketing, in which anyone with cash can reach millions of people, getting your message noticed by the head of IT at the Fortune 500 companies takes more than just cash.

Permission Marketing isn't about the interruption part of the process. You're still going to figure out how to reach out and get their attention once. But once you've got someone's attention (especially that rare someone who's a qualified prospect), don't you dare let it go!

The most common question business-to-business marketers ask us is how they can use our tools to reach qualified prospects that are not currently talking with them. Unfortunately there is no magic bullet. The frequency techniques that make Permission Marketing so effective don't remove the need for Interruption Marketing. They don't eliminate the awkward and expensive moment that comes the first time you attempt to talk with a stranger. Marketers need to budget the money it takes to get the attention from these prospects using interruption techniques and then leverage that money over time.

Building a booth at a trade show, for example, isn't cheap. But how many companies build retention and attention programs that take the assets these trade shows create and really follow up on them? I know that I've swiped my badge through countless card readers at trade shows, and it's rare indeed if there's any follow-up at all. And I can't remember one instance where there was a consistent suite of follow-up messages.

I wrote a letter to a large industrial and athletic supply company that makes scoreboards and asked for more information on one of their products. What happened? Ideally I would have been enrolled in a Permission Marketing program that provided me with a suite of messages over time. An investment of energy on the part of the company to take me from stranger to friend and then friend to customer.

Instead they sent a brochure. No follow-up of any kind on a $10,000 potential sale. Some companies, if they're really aggressive, would have a low-level salesperson call to qualify me. But the organized, testable marketing presale is missing at most companies.

Permission Marketing should be the cornerstone of any business-to-business campaign that has a significant profit per customer. Building a base of qualified prospects is incredibly difficult, and not leveraging it is a sin.

3. When (and How) Should I Use the Web?

Lots of companies are on the Web for reasons that have nothing to do with marketing to prospects. The Web can offer substantial cost reductions, for example, when you allow a consumer to do work that your staff used to do.

You can also use the Web as a chance to publish information for external employees, partners, and existing customers. It's a great medium for Federal Express, for example, because allowing any customer instant access to their tracking database saves them time and money and also generates significant loyalty.

One major insurance company I work with is investing more than $20 million to build a Web site that will dramatically decrease their costs, but at the same time it will increase the length of time customers stay with them.

The trap most companies fall into is that they build a Web site for their existing, motivated customers and assume there's no problem turning that site into a customer acquisition tool as well.

Go to Microsoft.com and take a look at their home page. It's a disaster! (Hopefully, by the time you get there they'll have read this book and changed it.) First, it features news and information on an astonishing array of products for a wide assortment of users. Looking at it today, for example, I see news of a free update to their Web browser for consumers, a new enterprise-wide initiative for IT professionals, and half a dozen other tidbits. Who is this for? Won't most people, when faced with this odd assortment of data, just turn and flee?

And how many non-Microsoft customers will take the time to dig eight levels into the site to discover what they really need to know?

There's a different solution, and one that makes the Web much more functional as a marketing tool.

The first step is to have two sites, one for customers and one for prospects. The customer site ought to have a less likely name. In this case, for example, www.microsoftinfo.com would work great. After all, once someone is a customer, it's easy to teach him what your Web address is.

The second site is the front door to your marketing message. Regardless of why your company built a customer site on the Web, use permission throughout your prospect Web site. It's an almost free way to dramatically increase the effectiveness of your Web campaign.

The only goal of the prospect site should be to get permission to follow up. It should be a handful of pages long, and the entire focus should be to get the consumer to do two things: 1) tell you what he or she wants to know, what problem needs to be solved; and 2) give you permission to follow up by e-mail.

Once you grab this permission, you're on your way to a sale. Why? Because now you can use curriculum marketing to teach the prospect about what you have to offer. You can use interactivity to gain information about your prospects in a dialogue. You can deliver messages that are anticipated, personal, and relevant.

Once you've built a permission acquisition Web site that works, you need to drive people to it. You can do the math. For every one hundred people who arrive, x percent will give you permission. For every person who gives you permission, you'll generate $\$y$ in sales.

So the next step is to drive people to your acquisition site (not your customer site). The Web is horrible at reach. For this reason, you don't want to focus your prospect acquisition solely online unless your product revolves around the Net.

It's more effective to use the media you've already invested in to get permission and then to use that permission to deliver anticipated, personal, and relevant messages to prospects' e-mail boxes.

You'll get the best of both worlds. First, you'll take advantage of the huge reach that mass media offers. Second, you'll leverage that reach with the frequency you can get from the Internet.

Imagine a car company, for example, that's already running ads on TV. For free they can modify these ads to invite interested consumers to send e-mail to ford@chevy.com or whatever. They can entice them with a prize or with a rebate or with an offer of more information.

Do you think if Ford focused on this, they could collect 2 million permissions? Of course! And each one of the 2 million ensuing dialogues would certainly increase Ford's branding. And many, many of those dialogues would get personal. Which means that Ford could make them relevant. And turn them into dealer visits.

The marginal cost of this campaign by Ford is close to zero. They're already buying the TV time. The online costs are all fixed. Nothing but upside here. The challenge for a big company like Ford isn't the money. It's the coordination of the organization. How to get the TV people, the ad agencies, the new media people, the marketing group, and the dealers to all work together on a planned, focused effort. That's one reason that small companies are in the forefront of applying these techniques correctly. They're more agile and quicker to adapt to new trends that work better.

But isn't it inappropriate to run a sweepstakes to market to doctors, lawyers, or business professionals?

It may well be. But Permission Marketing isn't about games or sweepstakes. It's about taking a businesslike direct marketing approach to high-frequency, relevant, personal, and anticipated interactions with prospects.

If your base of doctors won't respond to the "bait" of a trip to France, perhaps they're more interested in getting the latest news about new drugs or getting updates on the latest golf tournaments.

Here's an example from a drug company in Massachusetts:

The biggest problem in launching a new drug after you've earned FDA approval is to get doctors to prescribe it. The pharmaceutical companies do this by hiring hundreds or thousands of sales reps to hit the road and meet with doctors.

If it's an important drug, it will be the only product the sales reps sell. At about $140,000 a year in salary, plus commissions and bonuses, you can see that this is an extraordinarily expensive undertaking.

The pharmaceutical companies need live salespeople because over time, a personal call evolves into a mild level of permission. The doctor comes to trust the salesperson and to expect and look forward to the information she brings.

This company, though, is now using e-mail to dramatically leverage the power of word of mouth to build acceptance of their drugs. The president of the company maintains a phone and e-mail correspondence with several of the most important doctors in this particular specialty.

These doctors, primarily researchers, can influence hundreds or thousands of other doctors. In this case, a brain surgeon asked for FDA data from the drug company. As a result of a long-term permission campaign, he already trusted the president of the company (and vice versa). So the president e-mailed the surgeon the actual PowerPoint presentation that was presented to the FDA—on the same day it was sent to the FDA.

The doctor was delighted to get the scoop. As a result of this directed marketing effort, he featured six of the slides verbatim during a presentation to 3,000 other brain surgeons in the most important conference in his field.

It doesn't matter what the bait is as long as it is relevant to your audience and enhances attention and responsiveness.

Just because someone is a professional doesn't mean he isn't selfish! Make yourself a little sign and post it on your wall. America's favorite radio station is still WII-FM (what's in it for me), and if you don't acknowledge that with the professionals you're interacting with, they won't give up their valuable time to respond.

4. Can Permission Marketing Help Our Branding?

What's branding, after all, but a stand-in for how much access you have to consumers? If I trust Ivory, I'm more likely to allow the company to sell me a shampoo—at least once—than I might be with an unknown brand.

If you have deep and regular permission with appropriate prospects, brand is useful but secondary in the decision-making process. Much more important is your access and your ability to personalize.

Take a look at the giant insurance companies. They have a giant asset—the personal relationships that their thousands of agents have with millions of customers and prospects. Everything else is a commodity.

This personal permission is quite valuable. And many

times there's a brand hung around it—a piece of the rock or the good hands people. The brand certainly helps the insurance broker have credibility, and the good work of the insurance broker makes the brand stronger still.

For many products that rely on branding, Permission Marketing may be overkill. For example, until Evian goes into the subscription water business, I'm not sure that a curriculum-based marketing effort is the best way for them to increase sales.

Companies with products that are low cost and that aren't necessarily going to benefit from a lifetime customer should continue to focus on Interruption Marketing to build their brand. They should not distract themselves with direct marketing, the Web, or loyalty programs. Instead they should be buying up all the available airspace that's being abandoned by big-ticket marketers.

Something else to think about: Virtually all branding money is totally wasted. Let's look at the math for a typical national magazine like *Time, Newsweek,* or *People:*

Cost of a full-page color ad: $50,000
Circulation: 3,000,000
Number of minutes spent per issue: 22
Number of ads per issue: 80

So even if there were no articles, that's sixteen seconds per ad. But we know that most people do read articles and don't read ads.

The percentage of people who can remember reading

your ad when they're done with the magazine: Your guess is as good as mine, but let's say 8 percent.

The percentage of those who read the ad and can recall what the ad said: 30 percent

The number of people who were impacted by the ad: 72,000.

So the cost of impacting each person once is about 80 cents.

Permission Marketing can't deliver that first audience of strangers any faster or cheaper than an ad can. But after that, it can deliver targeted permission-building messages for far less money. What if that 80 cents' worth of impact didn't end after one ad but got to be extended for weeks or months?

5. What's the Difference between Permission Marketing and What We're Doing Now?

Most marketers practice Interruption Marketing. The difference is simple. An Interruption Marketer is a hunter. A Permission Marketer is a farmer.

Hunting prospects involves loading a gun with bullets and shooting until you hit something. You can take a day or a week or a month off from this endeavor and it won't take you long to get back into successfully bagging a few.

Farming prospects involves hoeing, planting, watering, and harvesting. It's infinitely more predictable, but it takes regular effort and focus. If you take a month off, you might lose your entire crop. On the other hand, farming scales. Once you get good at it, you can plant ever more seeds and harvest ever more crops.

6. Why Can't We Sell the Names and Data We Collect?
My Company Has Been Doing This in Direct Marketing for Years,
and It's a Major Profit Center for Us.

Of course you can sell the data you collect. But the moment you do, you have devalued the permission you were granted.

True permission comes when you create a monogamous personal relationship with an individual. The individual is given the incentive to trust you and share ever more personal data in exchange for focused, relevant, personal marketing messages that save him time and money.

But once that data is shared and a third party enters the picture, the third party causes two things to happen:

1. The third party increases the clutter by 100 percent or more, thus sabotaging the private relationship you worked so hard to create.
2. The third party profits by violating the trust you created. The consumer is burned and, more often than not, flees.

Here are three thought tests. How would you react if they happened to you?

1. Your lawyer sells data about your company's status to a financial services company, which uses it to get access to you and to present a loan proposal. The company knows your salary, your cash flow, and all about the crises you are facing.

2. *Playboy* magazine buys data from the Book of the Month Club about which books you've bought. Based on the

data, they decide you might like their magazine and send you solicitations for it.

3. You enter a sweepstakes online and use your private e-mail address. The sweepstakes company sells your e-mail address to one hundred other companies, and suddenly you're receiving so much spam, you have to switch to another e-mail account (and you have to notify all your friends and colleagues about the switch).

In each case, you've been dramatically robbed of your incentive to give further permission to the marketer who rented your name. In each case, there's more clutter. In each case, the marketer sold herself short by taking a few pieces of silver today instead of leveraging the permission into long-term profits.

There's one exception to this principle: If you reward the consumer and receive in exchange overt, obvious opt-in, then by all means go ahead and share the name. Yoyodyne, for example, has an opt-in list in which we offer consumers a chance to tell us their interests so we can rent their names to marketers who choose to reach them by e-mail.

The consumers get two benefits: 1) they get more entries to win a prize; and 2) they receive information about things that match their profile.

About 38 percent of the people we present this offer to do, in fact, opt in. But this is very different from an opt-out campaign, in which consumer data is rented and used until the victim takes an action and opts out. Opt-out is a sham. It takes power away from the consumer and provides a flimsy opportunity for the marketer.

To be clear, opt-in is a specific election on the part of a consumer to participate. Opt-out means that the election is made for them automatically by the marketer, and only by actively choosing *not* to receive the messages can the consumer be left alone. The junk mail that clogs your mailbox at home is opt-out. You can stop it by writing to the Direct Marketing Association, but until you do, it's going to keep on coming.

Opt-out is a thin asset. Because consumers don't ask for it, it's unanticipated and usually irrelevant. That makes it far less effective.

Permission Marketers focus their energy on building long-term relationships in which power rests with the consumer. They realize that in the long run this can be the foundation for huge profits.

7. How Does the Power Shift When Permission Marketing Becomes More Prevalent?

"Paradigm shift" seems to be the phrase of the decade. But the fact is, the world is changing, and in a very profound way. It appears that there are going to be only two kinds of companies—the swift and the dead.

In every market, and with every audience, three things are demonstrably true:

1. Permission is a powerful asset, and it can be leveraged.
2. As the clutter gets worse and worse, permission is worth more and is harder to get.
3. In every market segment, only a limited number of companies will be able to secure permission.

So if we take a look at the race to build an online book-seller, we see that Amazon.com, Barnes & Noble, and soon Bertelsmann are all fighting a battle for permission. Each company is prepared to lose money on every new customer in a race to build a large and profitable permission base.

1. In the book business, the intermediary who acquires a great deal of permission will sell a lot of books, will gain more power with its suppliers, and will ultimately put the suppliers out of business by publishing books directly with the authors themselves.

2. In the book business, the low-hanging fruit is gone. The most likely online book buyers have already signed up with one service or another, so acquiring each new customer costs more.

3. In the book business, once a consumer has given permission to one provider, there's little need or incentive for him to add a second one to the roster. After Amazon.com has solved your "where do I go for books" problem, you're free to move on to your next problem. It's unlikely you'll spend much time switching around.

So there's a battle brewing. In every industry from mutual funds to groceries, just a few companies will end up with permission to market to a huge number of qualified customers. And when that happens, these companies—gatekeepers—will start to exert power.

These permission holders will begin by treating all their suppliers like commodities (and in many ways they are). Like all commodity suppliers, these companies will have to cut their prices (and their profits) in order to keep the business.

Wal-Mart does this with laundry detergent already. As the reseller of more than 25 percent of all the laundry detergent sold in the entire country, they have a huge amount of power. The consumer has given Wal-Mart situational permission to sell them detergent, and Wal-Mart gets to choose which brand. Wal-Mart's power over Procter & Gamble is formidable and getting bigger.

The implications here are substantial. Companies that aren't used to being the final step between the consumer and the product need to think long and hard about whether they wish to become gatekeepers or to build direct permission relationships with consumers. Companies like Procter or Colgate or Estée Lauder are having huge internal debates about channel conflict.

The channel conflict issue is simple—should you stick with your long-term retailers, or should you try to bypass them and go straight to the consumer?

Miss the opportunity to build a permission relationship directly with the consumer, and your company is likely to become a commodity supplier. If you acknowledge the coming power of the permission holder yet choose to avoid the battle to become one, you can still win. If you start now, you can optimize your company for the role of supplying the permission holder, making yourself more attractive to these gatekeepers and locking in the long-term relationships that can give you insulation moving forward.

On the other hand, if you go for the opportunity to deal direct, you'll face the wrath of your existing intermediaries. It'll be expensive to build and maintain a permission base, and risky too. But if you succeed, you will have built an asset that can offset the demands of the gatekeepers. You'll be able to maintain fair pricing and generate better profits.

The worst path is to try to do both (which is also the most likely path for established companies). By trying to serve two masters, you'll probably do neither job well. Company after company has floundered as it tried to build a direct relationship with consumers at the same time it tried hard not to offend the retailer or gatekeeper that initiated the original relationship.

For example, computer companies have traditionally relied on independent dealers and VARs (value-added resellers) to sell their computers to businesses and individuals. You couldn't just call up IBM or Digital and buy a laptop.

The channel conflict that might come if one of these companies attempts to build a serious direct-to-consumer marketing effort is significant. The dealers who represent the lifeblood of the company will switch to another supplier, causing all sorts of chaos in the marketplace.

Compaq, for example, is hindered in its Permission Marketing campaign because it doesn't want to alienate the existing channel. Dell has no channel and, as a result, is killing Compaq.

A few years ago Dell spent millions of dollars trying to do both. They thought they could leverage their direct relationship and turn it into a retail relationship as well. They failed dismally and were smart enough to retrench and focus on nothing but the end user.

Once a consumer begins as a Dell customer, Dell has permission to keep in touch. They know the name, the phone number, and the preferences of this customer. Compaq has no idea who its customers are. If Dell leverages the permission they've got, they ought to be able to turn these consumers into customers for life. And Compaq will have no chance to steal them away.

This seems pretty straightforward for the computer industry. But what about clothes (Levi's now sells jeans direct) or perfume or coffee or any number of products we're used to buying through a middleman? Every one of these brands faces the same challenge. Do they remain a manufacturer, beholden to the retailer, or do they take the plunge and become a gatekeeper?

Not everyone can become a gatekeeper, though. Perhaps American Airlines can live without travel agents, but SAS or Philippine Airways can't. Instead they'll have to focus on becoming a primary supplier for the aggregators that *do* become the gatekeepers of permission. Will they have to give up more and more of their margin in order to keep market share? Without a doubt.

8. If Permission Marketing Is So Effective, Why Does Interruptive TV Advertising Still Dominate the Marketing Landscape?

The main reason is habit. Nobody ever got fired for running a TV commercial, and the inertia here is huge. There are entire departments of companies, large ad agencies, and a media and production infrastructure that survive because of the huge sums spent in this area.

You can see just how ludicrous this strategy is when you look at Gardenburger. This product (which I happen to think is terrific) is a hamburger made out of vegetables. It was the offshoot of a failed restaurant, and it's managed to do respectable numbers in grocery stores and diners around the country.

The problem facing the folks at Gardenburger is that most people have never tasted one.

Their solution—TV advertising. To be specific, the company floated a bond and equity offering to fund a nationwide TV campaign. And instead of building an audience one person at a time by focusing on frequency and niche markets (ads on the Food Channel, for example, would go a long way toward reaching people most likely to experiment with food), the company bet virtually all the money on just one night. They bought two commercials on the last episode of Seinfeld, the most overpriced night of TV advertising in history, a showcase for big companies and big ads.

Gardenburger has taken TV advertising to its ultimate extreme. They bet a huge share of the company on the belief that two thirty-second advertisements would be sufficient to get people's attention, build trust, and encourage trial.

According to *The Wall Street Journal*, the effect of the campaign was primarily to benefit Gardenburger's bigger competitors. It drove people to the category, and once they got there, they chose the most convenient offering.

It doesn't matter if the campaign pays for itself or not. What's clear is that the same money spent in a permission-focused campaign would do better. But the allure and ease of a TV campaign clouded the company's vision.

You'll notice that the people who really measure marketing results—direct marketers like the Columbia Record Club and Spiegel—never advertise on network TV. There's a reason. It doesn't pay.

Will big-budget TV advertising work for some brands? Without a doubt. Lifestyle brands with less of a story—things like beer or beverages or even batteries—can really benefit from this emotional connection. But for most businesses, it just isn't worth what it costs unless there's a back-end component as well.

9. How Important Is Testing?

When mass media works it's because it targets the masses cheaply. Permission Marketing can't do that. But what it can do is allow you to test. To test everything. Every day. To build hundreds of tests that don't require talent or genius, just perseverance.

You can't overestimate the value of this. Aggressively testing every element of a permission campaign can double or triple its effectiveness. Because permissioned communications are usually individual and private, a marketer can run one hundred of them at the same time. A mass marketer doesn't dare, for fear that it will completely confuse the marketplace.

Testing is a discipline. It's hard to get started, but once you set it up, it's much easier to run. You don't need endless meetings to determine the "right" creative solution. Run them all!

You should be testing the length, the pricing, the voice, the creative execution, the reward systems, the compression, the demographics of respondents—everything you can imagine.

And if your frequency vehicle is inexpensive, you should be testing the most outlandish things you can imagine. You should test jokes and family stories and 80 percent–off sales and "buy this product or we'll shoot this dog." This medium is designed for testing, and testing works best when you assume nothing.

10. What Should We Do with Our Existing Web Site?

I won't go as far as to tell you to shut it down, but you should move it immediately, and you should also stop investing so much time and money in making it miraculous and cool.

Your Web site for new prospects should be small and fast and simple. And it should collect e-mail addresses in exchange for a promise of a benefit.

Once you collect that data, care for it. Upgrade. Learn more. Send people to specific sections of your existing Web site. Give them a reason to go there.

One business-to-business company we work with is actively considering hiring fifty people to do nothing but answer e-mail that they collect on their Web site. The cost of caring for prospects in this way is far lower than any other sales technique they've examined.

If you get a chance, check out www.ge.com. General Electric's Web site, built at some ungodly cost, is perhaps the worst example of a big company's establishing a committee and then burning its cash.

What conceivable reason is there to believe that a consumer will be motivated enough to dive five or ten levels deep into a Web site to find the toll-free number for GE Capital's mortgage refinance division? Or that nuclear power plants and refrigerators belong on the same home page?

The alternative is so simple. Tell us your name and what you want to know, and we'll look up the answer and write back to you within one minute! The site should exist only to encourage prospects to actually fill out the form.

The end result is permission from the consumer and the beginning of a long-term permission relationship.

There's room for brochureware. But focus on permission first.

11. What Are the Biggest Stumbling Blocks Companies Face?

The first is organizational. You're probably not organized for Permission Marketing, and there are many, many entrenched special interests that will stand in your way. In many ways, the dawn of Permission Marketing and the birth of the Web have thrown big companies into a panic and led to a long, painful rebirth.

The second is greed. Once the seeds of permission are planted, there's going to be huge pressure to harvest the results right away. But the sooner you begin to leverage this base, the less it will grow. Giving is far more important than taking, especially at the beginning.

Imagine how much less successful the frequent flier programs would have been if they'd been as jammed with partners, restrictions, and special offers as they are today.

Patience is critical when building these programs.

The third is foresight. It's much easier to hunt for a customer when you get to make it up as you go along. The planning and prebuilt suites required for a permission campaign mean your organization has to be disciplined enough to plan ahead. It's harder than it sounds, especially the first few times.

What are the first steps to take to get started with Permission Marketing?

You can walk before you run. In order, here's what you should do:

1. Figure out the lifetime value of a new customer. Without this data it will be extremely difficult to compute what it's worth to acquire a new permission.

2. Invent and build a series of communication suites that you will use to turn strangers into friends. This can be a series of e-mails, a series of letters, a number of scripts to use in phone conversations, a series of Web pages, and so on. Essential to each suite are four elements:

   - They must take place over time.
   - They must offer the consumer a selfish reason to respond.
   - The responses should alter the communications moving forward (change the message as you learn more about the consumer).
   - They should have a final call to action so you can measure the results.

3. Change all of your advertising to include a call to action. Never run an ad of any kind that doesn't give consumers a chance to respond. Once they respond, initiate one of the communication suites.

4. Measure the results of each suite. Throw out the bottom 60 percent and replace them with new suites. Continue testing different approaches forever.

5. Measure how many permissions you achieve. Measure how much permission changes buying behavior. Reward all parties on the permission team for exceeding metrics.

6. Assign one person to guard the permission base. Have that person focus on increasing the level of permission gained from each individual and reward her for resisting short-term profiteering.
7. Work to decrease your cost of frequency by automating responses and moving to e-mail and the Internet.
8. Rebuild your Web site to turn it from brochureware to a focused permission acquisition medium.
9. Regularly audit your permission base to determine how deep your permission really is.
10. Leverage your permission by offering additional products or services or by co-marketing with partners.

Acknowledgments

It's really hard to have a big idea and not have the words to talk about it. Yoyodyne gave me the space, the energy, the motivation, and the laboratory to put this idea into practice and eventually into words. Special thanks to a core group of folks who gave up safe jobs with safe companies to change the world: David Simon, Dan Lovy, Marc Fogel, Mike Dubin, Dev Bhatia, Chris Jones, Anne Shepherd, Meg Smith, Susan Storms, Wendy Hall, and dozens of other very smart, very motivated marketers, salespeople, engineers, and producers who have influenced the way we approach this market. I'm wrong more often than I'm right, and it takes guts to prove it. These guys did.

The money and the big advice came from my illustrious board, including Lester Wunderman, the father of direct marketing; Tom Cohen, who believed in the vision first; Larry Miller, who took a gamble; and the extraordinary pair of Fred Wilson and Jerry Colonna. Fred and Jerry are perhaps the smartest, most honest, and most productive venture capitalists I've had the pleasure to meet.

Special thanks to the estimable Randy Rodman, who

worked with me from the beginning to make this book a reality. Randy's insights and research were invaluable.

Don Peppers and Martha Rogers didn't know what they were getting me into when they wrote their seminal book, *The One to One Future,* but it has been a guiding light for the work we've done at Yoyodyne. Don has given me plenty of time and support and insight, and I've enjoyed working with the irrepressible Bob Dorf as well.

The book itself wouldn't have existed without the help of my muse, Lisa DiMona. Sometimes you get lucky. I did. And of course, at the core of everything I've ever had to say about marketing sits Jay Levinson, the father of guerrilla marketing, my friend, and a legitimate genius. Sitting next to him is Lisa Gansky, a brilliant and kind mensch who knows more about marketing online than anyone (and fortunately, she's on our team).

Special thanks to Fred Hills, who is willing to take a book by the hand and make it better. And to Karen Watts and Robin Dellabough, who have been there from the start.

INDEX